When Leo Logged On

A True Tale of Pop Culture
and the Dawn of the Digital Age

A Memoir by Susan Ashbaine

Events, timelines, and dialogue reflect the author's recollection and have been adapted for narrative clarity. Names, locations, and identifying details of private individuals have been changed to protect privacy. Composite characters combine traits from multiple people from different times and locations, and are not intended to depict any one identifiable person. Public figures are portrayed from public record and firsthand experience. Individuals presented to the author as anonymous are not claimed to have been definitively identified.

1st edition 2025

V1.006

For my favorite Teletubby

Contents

Preface

I flopped into the chair in front of the bank of monitors I'd spent the last two years staring at for eight hours a day, an organized mess of computer equipment that included both my day job and home office gear. After powering down the work laptop for the weekend, I turned to my personal machine and, with a weary sigh, opened a blank document.

The night before, I'd been unpacking the 25-year-old memories I'd kept hidden from anyone who might mock or doubt them, myself included. Those ruminations ignited a flash of inspiration: the story of how my life and career unfolded was downright ordinary, until you consider that an anonymous chat room visitor in 1999 changed everything. I wasn't sure if it would sound lame or incredible to anyone else, but I decided I wanted to find out.

I'd always known every thread led back to what should have been just another typical night at the movies. *Titanic* was the first film I had ever seen that left me feeling unsettled for hours after I left the theater. Years later, I realized a butterfly had flapped its wings that night, nudging my life in an entirely unexpected direction.

I had been captivated by the haunted romance of *RMS Titanic*'s story ever since the wreck was discovered in 1985, when I was just 11 years old. I had even written a research paper on the theories surrounding the sinking for a high school English class a few years later. When I saw the earliest promos for the James Cameron film in 1997, I mistook the blonde boy in the poster for Jonathan Taylor Thomas, whom I struggled to picture as a dramatic romantic lead, but I was still excited at the prospect of a modern take on the tragedy brought to life on the big screen.

Given how deeply invested I was in this piece of history, it took months after watching the film to realize that the despair I felt as I left the theater that day had little to do with the devastation that had unfolded on the screen. It had come from something far more personal. It came from seeing my own reflection in the character of Rose DeWitt Bukater.

I had gone to see *Titanic* less than two years after I suffered a loss that left me feeling as unmoored as those lifeboats drifting in the North Atlantic. I hadn't realized the desperation to find some kind of anchor had led me down a path I never would've chosen otherwise. Watching Rose's narrow escape from her gilded cage helped me see that I'd been quietly flailing, pretending to be happy when what I really wanted was someone to throw me a lifeline, to pull me back from the life I had chosen too hastily. I wanted my own Jack Dawson.

Enter stage left: Leonardo DiCaprio.

Preface

Between 1997 and 1999, "Leomania" spread like wildfire, fueled by the shockwave of an exploding internet. It's difficult to convey just how overwhelming it was to anyone who grew up amid behemoth fan ecosystems like the Swifties or the BeyHive. For that brief moment in time, Leo became a white-hot supernova, commanding everyone's attention with blinding force. One might compare Leomania to the great *Titanic* herself: massive and iconic, but short-lived and built for a different time. It couldn't rival the scale or structure of Taylor Swift's modern cruise ship of a fandom, but it struck just as deep an emotional chord.

In the absence of social media, the young internet of the day became awash with hundreds of Leo- and *Titanic*-themed fan pages, built by fledgling webmasters from every corner of the globe. Buried deep in that digital quagmire was an unassuming message board that held the key to my next secret. It is the one that, to this day, the few people I've dared tell this tale to insist was one of the earliest cases of what we now call celebrity catfishing.

I know exactly how it sounds. I've rolled my eyes at other people making similar claims more times than I can count.

I'll admit that part of my motivation for writing this book is to document every piece of proof I can recall from that time, to lay out my case for you, the judge, and maybe one day, get direct confirmation from an indisputable source. Despite my unyielding confidence in what I experienced over 25 years ago and my belief in my own ability to discern truth from deception, there will always be a persistent voice in the back of my mind asking, *What if?*

What if it really was all an elaborate ruse, an impeccably timed hoax?

Yet, in all my searching, in all my relentless pursuit of a standard of proof high enough to satisfy even my own skepticism, I have never found a single piece of evidence to contradict the assertion that, at the height of his *Titanic* fame, I was briefly an internet acquaintance of a newly minted A-list actor who trusted me implicitly to create a safe space online where he could commune with his fans in private.

More importantly, I could not have known at the time that this experience, real or not, would set the course for the rest of my life.

Chapter 1: Choose Your Adventure

"Why don't you understand what I'm asking you for?"

The man on the other end of the line sounded exasperated, mistaking his own confusion for my stupidity. "Every washer has a lint trap. Mine is missing. I need a replacement. This is not difficult."

I took a deep breath. This wasn't my first battle of wills with a customer who was absolutely, 100% wrong but absolutely, 100% unwilling to accept it.

"Sir, washing machines don't have lint traps. Are you thinking of a drain filt—"

"No. No. *No*," he interrupted. "I know what I'm talking about! Every washer I've ever owned has had one. Maybe you should get your supervisor to find it. I'm sure *he* knows what I'm talking about."

I sneered at the computer screen, resisting the urge to bang my head against the desk. Calls like this were routine at the appliance call center, a never-ending battle between reality and whatever version of it the customer had decided was true.

My job was simple: type in the appliance model number to pull up a list of available parts, but if the part the caller wanted wasn't listed, quite often I was told to "find a man" who apparently would be able to make it appear.

The call center sat in a sprawling, single-story office park on the west side of Knoxville, Tennessee, one of many nearly identical red-brick buildings that housed operations just like it. These clusters of daytime destinations turned West Knoxville into a traffic nightmare at rush hour. Those who had experienced both liked to call it "Little Atlanta," a nod to the treacherous gridlock Metro Atlanta has always been notorious for. In 1998, I was one of those young professionals trudging through the daily traffic jams that clogged the roadways, slowly making my way to a job on a side of town I'd never be able to afford to live in.

I had grown up on the north side of town, three miles past the last convenience store, tucked deep into the gentle, rolling Appalachian foothills of East Tennessee. It had been a wonderful place to be a child, surrounded by woods on the side of a ridge with a creek winding through the valley below. But living that far into the countryside as an adult made commuting across the city each day a crawling, frustrating slog.

Within the call center, the parts department occupied a small corner of the wide open workspace. The rest of the building was a cubicle farm full of large, semi-enclosed cubes occupied by staff dedicated to appliance sales in one form or another. As peddlers of mere appliance parts, however, my teammates and I were relegated to the smallest desks in the building. Ours were a single row of narrow cubicles, each just wide enough to accommodate the bulky CRT monitors that were still standard in those days. The dividers that extended only two feet above the desktop were all that offered even an illusion of privacy.

I kept my cube walls cluttered with company-branded promotional items, but one item stood out from among the corporate swag. It was a single, proudly displayed movie ticket stub from the night I first saw *Titanic* back in February of that year. I was not typically one to save such remnants, but I imagined looking back on it in years to come much like those lucky enough to have seen another historic production that I had been enamored with, *Gone With the Wind*, during its first release.

Fortunately, I got along well with my closest cubicle neighbors. To my right was Stacey, a bright and easygoing woman in her mid-20s with a Sheryl Crow vibe; effortlessly cool and laid-back, the kind of girl I'd always aspired to be. To my left was Josh, a blonde-haired, 20-year-old college student with that elusive "popular kid" charm, never lacking in wisecracks. Handsome and goofy in equal measure, he had a knack for pushing his pranks just a little too far, often skirting the fine line between funny and infuriating.

"Chi-coe-nay," I enunciated slowly, peering around the divider into Stacey's cube.

A friend had called her desk phone, and since our caller ID ran through the computer terminal, his name had popped up on her screen in large enough text for me to see from my seat. Unluckily for her, *she* had a nosy cube neighbor.

"Wow," I heard him say through her headset. "Nobody ever says Ciccone correctly."

We were packed in so closely I could hear every word. I grinned mischievously. I had a secret weapon. Not only did I know Ciccone was Madonna's last name, but my high school choir teacher had taught us pronunciation rules for several languages, Italian included, so I rarely got names wrong. It was the only gift I had that consistently worked to my benefit in the call centers.

Stacey barely glanced at me, raising a single sassy eyebrow before turning back to her screen.

The supervisors, who spent most of their day monitoring our mostly boring calls and suppressing their giggles at the more ridiculous ones, sat in a circular desk formation at the end of our row. Among them was my boss, Dan, a rotund, middle-aged man who found the snark borne from my lack of customer service skills absolutely hysterical. Sharon, his counterpart overseeing the other half of our section, did not share in his amusement.

The work itself was so monotonous that Dan and Sharon encouraged their teams to bring books to read whenever call volume slowed to a trickle. Many of us kept well-worn paperbacks tucked into drawers or propped open on our desks. Some read novels, others flipped through magazines, and a few even brought textbooks, using any available time to cram for college classes at the nearby University of Tennessee.

In early 1998, there was no such thing as browsing the internet to fill downtime between calls, at least not in this office. The call center's computers were "dumb terminals,"[2] running a primitive DOS-based menu system with a text-driven interface that had all the ease of a tax form. There was no mouse or windows to click through, just a blinking cursor and a long list of function keys to memorize.

I started working there just before a major system upgrade replaced those ancient computers with sleek new Windows 95 machines in mid-1998. The old amber-on-black screens became instantly obsolete, replaced by vibrant, full-color monitors that greeted us with the unmistakable solid teal default desktop, revealed only after jiggling the mouse to disengage the flying starfield screensaver, of course.

With the new machines, unfettered access to the rapidly expanding World Wide Web had finally arrived. Always-on internet felt like a forbidden indulgence by comparison to home dial-up service. To our surprise, we were given the all-clear to put down our books and surf the web with abandon so long as we paid attention when the phones rang.

Some of the staff were nervous using a Windows machine for the first time, but I had been waiting for this moment. Until then, the majority of my computing experience had been with machines that were incapable of internet access, but that didn't mean I was unfamiliar with technology.

In fact, I had been navigating computers long before most of my coworkers ever touched a keyboard. My earliest introduction to technology had come a full 14 years earlier, through the TRS-80 Color Computer and later the Commodore 64 brought into our home by my father. I was just 10 years old when my father bartered his way into our first TRS-80, a shiny gray box that looked more like a cash register than a gateway to the future. From the moment it entered our home, I was enthralled.

While other girls had sleepovers and played with their Barbies, I spent my evenings and weekends hunched over chunky books filled with pre-written BASIC programs. I sat there for hours, painstakingly copying lines of code onto the keyboard with laser focus, smacking the side of the 13-inch black-and-white television my father had repurposed as a monitor when a single out of place character caused an entire page of code to fail.

Without the separately sold floppy drive, the only way to save all that manually typed code was onto cassette tape. Our desk was cluttered with Memorex cases scrawled with handwritten labels, mixed in with tapes we had plucked out of Radio Shack's sale bins. One of those bargain cassettes held a game that eventually became the bane of my Saturday existence, indelibly imprinted in my memory.

Madness and the Minotaur was a text-based adventure game similar to the one young Josh Baskin plays on his computer in the movie *Big*. Each screen of text represented one of 256 "rooms" in an expansive castle-and-dungeon-style maze.

"YOU ARE IN A GREAT STONE TOWER WITH A LOW BROKEN CEILING AND A POOL OF WATER IN THE CORNER. A GRAND ARCHWAY IS ON THE EAST WALL."

It was the first of a long string of games that I would find more frustrating than fun. Instead of finding my way to freedom, I spent countless Saturdays wandering the maze in circles, stumbling into the same room with the same pool of water over and over again.

Not content with leaving the machine on the family dining table, my father handcrafted a wooden computer desk for our living room, building a custom monitor stand to hold that old TV set at just the right height. This machine was going to be something important, even if we didn't know it yet.

My father was a blue-collar worker and the father of four girls: Ginger, Robin, Jo Ann, and the youngest, me. My mother stayed home with us until I graduated into middle school, when she took a cashier job at a bookstore. Their meager paychecks never stretched far, but they were as resourceful as they were hardworking.

Fascinated by technology, my father considered Radio Shack one of his favorite haunts on payday, after our mother provided him with his weekly allowance from the family budget. More often than not, however, he operated through trade, offering his skills as a mechanic, welder, machinist, electronics repairman, or carpenter in exchange for such treats. If a neighbor had an old piece of equipment they no longer used, chances were good my father could fix whatever was wrong with it, and in doing so, bring some new technological wonder into our home. Generation X kids might be known for spending their afternoons playing Atari or some random off-brand gaming console, but my family had computers and we never noticed the difference.

When our TRS-80 arrived, it caused quite the stir in our household. Jo Ann, the sister closest in age to me, fought over computer time with the same fervor as we once had over Saturday morning cartoons. The older girls, however, were already older teenagers who bounced between whatever extracurricular activities they had chosen that semester, showing little interest in what appeared to be a toy.

I graduated high school in 1993 and within a year, Jo Ann had laid claim to the family computer when our father upgraded the TRS-80 to a Tandy 1000, moving the handmade desk into her bedroom, where access was granted strictly at her discretion. Without the screen time to learn its quirks, I grew timid around its Personal Deskmate menu interface, and became easily flustered by the newfangled graphical fly-out menus I was always getting lost in.

The Tandy 1000 felt like a high-tech luxury compared to the TRS-80. It was our first computer that came as a complete, polished set, with a matching color monitor that finally released the old black-and-white TV into my sole custody for late-night television viewing in my room. It was the one consolation I was granted for losing easy access to the computer.

In rapid succession, we upgraded again, this time to our first internet-capable Windows 3.1 machine. The noisy dial-up modem granted us access to the crude, text-heavy message boards hosted by Prodigy, an early internet service that helped pave the way for the World Wide Web we know today. We could send what we now know as emails, but only to other Prodigy users. It was just enough internet access for me and my friends to invite disaster, posting "hello out there" messages and waiting, with bated breath, for a private reply from some unknown entity lurking in the void. No one knew about online predators or scammers in those blissful, innocent days.

It felt like we'd gone from tinkering with a DIY gaming system to starring in an '80s sci-fi movie, featuring kids easily hacking into an online government mainframe. For the first time, we could finally reach beyond the walls of our house into the digital world, only to discover it was still mostly empty.

I much preferred to spend my limited computer time immersed in a 16-bit game of *King's Quest V*, though I was disgracefully bad at that game, too. It was infamous for its obscure puzzles, to the point that large guidebooks were published just to help players make sense of its logic. Even then, solving its riddles felt like an impossible feat without divine intervention, or at least a friend who had already beaten it.

Now, sitting in front of a brand-new color monitor attached to a new Windows 95 computer at my latest call center job, I thought of my father. He would have been spellbound by these machines, just as he had been with every technological leap before them, even though they are archaic by today's standards. For a moment, I was transported to a weekend two years earlier, in the spring of 1996 when I was not quite 22 years old.

The four of us girls had descended upon our country home that Easter to celebrate the first birthday of my parents' first grandchild. I had just moved back in after my first failed attempt at independence and the older girls had come to stay for the weekend. It was a full house, and the first time all six of us had been together in at least two years. Though he was the reserved sort who never said it outright, my mother later told us how proud my father was to have us all under one roof again, if only for a little while.

A week later, on the evening before his own birthday, he spent the day in the driveway lowering a new engine into a full-size Chevy pickup truck. He planned to sell it to cover the cost of replacing the flooring in our house as a gift for my mother. Taking on side projects like that was often how he scraped together the funds for home improvements. It was dangerous work but he did it alone, relying only on an engine hoist borrowed from a friend.

My father would only ask for help when a task was truly impossible to do alone, and there was remarkably little he couldn't manage by himself. There was no better example of this than when he designed and built our house, a two-story brick structure that seemed far too ambitious for one man, by rallying weekend help from my uncles and grandfather.

One of my favorite photos of him, now long gone, showed him alone at the site before the foundation was poured, sloshing through what can only be described as a mud pit, carrying a single two-by-four. My mother hadn't meant to capture anything profound when she snapped the photo, but as comedic as it looked, the image ended up saying everything about his humble determination and tireless work ethic.

My earliest memory as a child was of delivering red bricks from the pallets stacked in the back yard to my father, placing them on the pulley system he rigged up to lift them to his perch on the scaffolding he installed in front of the house. I was just two years old when we moved in and couldn't have brought more than one or two bricks per trip, but I was proud to be of assistance. I lived there for most of my first 23 years.

That night, after fastening the last engine mount in the Chevy and taking a shower, he planted himself in his favorite chair in the living room to watch a little TV before bed. As I passed through the room headed out for a late-night shopping trip to spend the first paycheck I'd earned since moving back home, he asked what I was going out to get. "Stuff," I mysteriously replied. He grinned impishly.

"Everybody's gotta have their stuff," he said, referencing his favorite George Carlin routine, *A Place for My Stuff.*

I realized later that smile had come from a happy mistake. That paycheck was the first one I'd had free in almost a year without rent, utilities, and groceries to gobble it up before I ever even saw a cent. My excitement for finally having the money to indulge a little had caused me to forget it was his birthday the next day. He went to bed convinced I'd raced out on a last minute mission for a birthday surprise.

By the time I returned, the house was darkened and still. I tiptoed back to my room and lay awake watching *I Love Lucy* on low volume, two rooms away from my parents' bedroom. The next sound I heard was my mother running down the hall, screaming.

My father suffered a massive heart attack in his sleep that night and was gone before he ever got the chance to see what the internet would become.

He was just 58 years old.

Chapter 2: Heel, Toe, Do-Si-Do

Many people who manage to escape high school with a friend group intact end up with a story of dramatic unraveling. If my own circle in 1995 had been a movie, the final act would have climaxed at a rare drunken party, complete with a late-night confrontation and belongings piled on the porch by morning, a cinematic signal that the villain had finally been cast out. A quiet scene of reflection among the survivors the following day would have wrapped the story in a neat little bow, just before the credits rolled.

I had kept to myself through school, preferring the company of one or two close, trusted friends, but I was inducted into a larger crowd late in my senior year. It was a loose-knit bunch initially formed out of the school's choir kids that somehow carried over into young adulthood. A core crew emerged that I jokingly called the country-fried version of *Friends*, with the small bungalow my friend Angie's parents purchased in 1993 standing in for the "big apartment" where anyone could drop in at any time.

I wanted to see myself as the Rachel Green of the group, someone with a lot more main character energy than I possessed. I hadn't yet accepted the reality that I was more of a Monica Geller, at least in terms of personality. Her line from the show, "Rules are good! Rules help control the fun," perfectly captured my modus operandi, much to the annoyance of my friends. The role of Rachel really belonged to Angie. It was only fitting. Though she was the youngest of our group, she was the outspoken one who had run out and gotten "The Rachel" haircut, along with thousands of other young women our age.

I never got the privilege of living in the house, but by the spring of 1995, there were a couple of girls I had never been close with locked in a battle for the role of Phoebe. Once one of them had moved in with Angie's family after a falling-out with her former roommates, the games were on. One of those contenders took the competition a little too far, causing resentment and jealousy to build up until it finally detonated like a bomb beneath the floorboards.

Once the storm passed, I realized something I should have seen all along. I was never really one of them. I had spent years forcing myself into spaces where I was merely tolerated, content to believe presence equated to belonging. I had been praised for my steadfast loyalty in the wake of the meltdown, yet after the final scene played out, no one reached for me. I just drifted out of their lives, seemingly without notice.

That year had been fraught on multiple fronts. It *started* with hope and promise. I had moved out of my parents' house for the first time and landed a new job making significantly more money than I ever had before. With the security of a healthy paycheck and my father's co-signature on the loan, I bought my first brand-new car, a 1995 Chevrolet Cavalier in bright red. It was a base model with manual windows and a blank panel where the radio should have been, but after years of driving the old beaters my father pieced together that often left me stranded, I was over the moon. That sense of excitement wouldn't last very long.

A friend had recommended me for a job at the large finance company where she worked, not far from the appliance call center where I'd eventually land. Per the typical office protocol, I started my new job on a Monday, a day that seemed to go spectacularly well. The job only required simple sorting of incoming mail and basic data entry. It was so simple, in fact, I had to force myself to slow down just to have enough work to last the whole day.

The section I worked in included three other ladies in a small cubicle alcove with an unobstructed view of the windows across the front of the building. The supervisor was an unapproachable woman who hid in a private office about 30 feet away, where I had only seen her during the interview. Now I was being trained by the team lead, Becky, a woman in her late 20s who sat two cubicles down from my new desk.

Becky and the other teammates had been on their best behavior the first two days, pausing to announce break and lunch times so the new girl wouldn't feel left out, waiting for me to finish what I was working on so I could join them. It seemed like we were getting along well, until Wednesday morning.

Traffic to West Knoxville was usually bad, but that day it was a complete snarl, and I arrived to work 15 minutes late. I rushed in, apologized for the delay, and jumped straight into my work, barely registering the scowl on Becky's face.

It wasn't until lunchtime that I noticed something was off, when I looked up and realized the whole team had all left without me. I'm not sure why I didn't immediately connect the two, except that I refused to believe they would have such a sharp reaction to something out of my control. I just kept quiet and focused on my work, hoping the hostility would burn itself out.

I had already figured out the work rhythm and adjusted my pace to finish everything on my desk right at 5 p.m., but getting my work done on time was a mistake. As I stood up to leave, Becky grumbled, "Weren't you *late* today?"

"Oh, of course, you're right, I forgot," I said, my voice tinged with embarrassment as I sat back down and pressed the power button on my monitor. But try as I might, I couldn't make more work appear. I simply had nothing to do until the mail cart came back around the next morning to bring me the next day's mail to data-enter.

I pretended to work for 15 minutes, shuffling files around in folders on my desk and typing into documents I didn't save. It was a ridiculous performance with an audience of one, but the ire I'd been on the receiving end of for no clear reason was just as disproportionate.

The rest of the week continued in much the same way. The entire team had become icy, like a switch had been flipped. It had become obvious they had all collectively decided I did not fit in with them, so I just kept my distance and silently went on with my work until Friday morning.

When I arrived to work that day, I saw my supervisor for the first time since the interview, standing next to my desk. I assumed she wanted to check in, to see how my first week had gone. She led me to her darkened office and closed the door behind us, motioning for me to sit in the guest chair facing her desk.

"I've been told you've refused to work the hours you're assigned," she said with a steely coldness. "This isn't going to work out. I'll need you to turn in your badge and leave immediately."

I was so shocked I didn't even defend myself. She hadn't even asked for my side of the story, but I had the feeling she wasn't interested in my point of view.

"I... I don't know what to say," was all I could manage to spit out before dropping my badge into her outstretched hand and walking out without another word. As I passed by the cubes where my now former team sat, Becky's eyes followed my walk of shame, her face gleaming with malevolent satisfaction.

For a long time, I thought Becky had just been looking for an excuse to replace me with someone she liked better. On second thought, maybe she was just a clock-watcher, the kind who gets outraged if someone is even a minute late. Perhaps she had believed I had come in much later on Wednesday than I had and was convinced I defiantly left early even after being reminded. All I knew at the time was that one simple mistake had brought down the guillotine blade.

My stomach twisted into knots as I walked across the parking lot toward the brand-new car I now had no way to pay for.

I scrambled to find work and had to settle for a job that paid far less than I had budgeted for. While I had grown up in a humble household, this was a level of financial strain I had never personally experienced. Determined to keep my car while preventing my father from taking a credit rating hit, I cut costs wherever I could, living on potatoes and 25-cent frozen pot pies while my paycheck barely kept the lights on.

By early spring 1996, I had to concede defeat and move back home. Two weeks later, my father, the rock I had learned to depend upon, was dead. And, I was alone. My friends gathered around me for his funeral, but evaporated into thin air as soon as it was over. For many of them, that would be the last time I ever saw them.

My father and I had never been terribly close. He was a typical Silent Generation father, strict in his gender roles, leaving child-rearing to my mother and stepping in primarily as a disciplinarian when needed. But if I ever found myself in trouble, he was always the first to show up.

Car accident? Call Dad.
Need help moving a friend? Call Dad.
Need to bury a cheating boyfriend's body? Call Dad.

At 21, that sense of security felt unshakable, something I assumed would always be there. And then, without warning, it wasn't. Without it, I felt completely adrift.

My friends and I had not been the partying type, at least not in our early 20s. With a few notable exceptions (including the night everything imploded), we stuck to sober social gatherings or hung out at the "big apartment" house when Angie's family was usually there. It wasn't out of character that a year earlier, her father had allowed her to go to the local 18-plus country dance club for her 18th birthday, as long as he could come along to keep her safe. I looked forward to singing karaoke for the first time, so I tagged along.

I did a lot of *tagging along* in those days.

The familiarity of the club from that earlier visit gave me the confidence to attend a line dance class there alone after my friends were gone and I had no one to accompany me. After class, I settled into a corner with a single beer, mindful of the drive home.

Half-hidden in the dim light of a seating area styled like a country front porch, I watched the dancers twirl and stomp across a large oval dance floor encircled by fencing meant to resemble a corral. It reminded *me* more of a skating rink than a dance floor in a club, thanks to the weekends I spent at Skatetown in my preteen years.

Only a few minutes had passed before a man around 30 years old approached me. He wore brown cowboy boots, tight blue jeans, and a brightly colored Western button-down shirt with pearl snaps. His big Stetson was pulled low over his forehead, casting a shadow across his face that made it almost impossible to make out his features. He looked like a '90s Garth Brooks wannabe.

He introduced himself as Gary and offered his hand. As he led me onto the floor for a mixer dance while Tim McGraw wailed from the corner speakers, I hesitated. The floor was already filling with couples lining up, two by two, preparing for the next song to begin.

I called out over the music, "But I don't know it!"

"I'll show you," he assured me.

When the music began, he guided me through the steps just once before I was spun around and into the arms of the next man in line. I was a bit mortified at first, but I caught on easily and kept the small talk to a minimum as I moved through the circle of enthusiastic dancers. Each time I was released to the next partner, I made sure to steal a glance at my original one, keeping track of him through the crowd until the song finally ended.

I have to remember what he's wearing, I thought to myself. I couldn't have picked him out of a lineup otherwise.

He dances weird, was my next thought, watching him sway against unfamiliar women, hunched over with his knees practically glued together as his hips gyrated. It looked a little sleazy, almost like he was mocking his own dance moves.

It's hard to gauge the measure of a man from inside a honky-tonk, especially when you're shouting over "Boot Scootin' Boogie" and "The Macarena." Before the night was over, I had barely managed to glean that he had temporarily moved in with his parents in Kingston, Tennessee, a small town west of Knoxville, while he looked for work.

It wasn't convenient, but far be it from me to judge a man for moving back home to get back on his feet, when I had just done the same.

His family was originally from Murfreesboro, Tennessee, a city southeast of Nashville. Since he didn't know anyone in town besides his parents, I agreed to meet him again the next weekend at the same club. From there, we settled into a routine of weekend dates, meeting halfway between our homes. But with both of us having recently moved back in with our parents, the lack of privacy rapidly became a problem. Almost haphazardly, we decided to move in together.

Had I not already known it was a mistake, I would have figured it out soon enough.

Fumbling to find stability after losing my father, I willingly ignored a barrage of flashing neon warning signals, including a painfully obvious mismatch in lifestyles. I brushed it aside because no one was challenging me. Witnessing my determination, my family stayed silent, neither offering support nor objection. I chose to interpret their silence as tacit approval.

While my new live-in boyfriend was at least willing to accompany me to movies and events he had no real interest in or grasp of, I don't recall a single insightful conversation between us beyond swapping past experiences. Gary had a simplistic view of life, satisfied to merely fulfill society's expectations to bring in any honestly earned paycheck, with no real hobbies or interests outside of watching baseball.

When we met, he had been working entry-level blue-collar jobs while studying for his commercial driver's license. By the time we moved in together, he had taken a job as a long-haul truck driver, leaving me alone for two-week stretches at a time. As an introvert, I welcomed the solitude. Where I should have seen overt incompatibilities, I made excuses. Where others would have found deal breakers, I found justifications.

Although the worst red flags didn't fully surface until much later, it was clear from the start the relationship wouldn't last. It was never more obvious than the day I planned a romantic welcome-home dinner after one of his first work trips.

I had everything timed perfectly. My homemade lasagna would come out of the oven the second he pulled into the driveway. It was a rare treat, since I almost never cooked. Mellow jazz drifted softly through the house and candlelight danced across the kitchen and living room. The scene was set for a perfect romantic evening.

I met Gary at the door, offering a glass of wine as he stepped into the ambiance I had so meticulously crafted. He greeted me with his usual light kiss, then walked past me without acknowledging the glass in my hand, tossing his dirty laundry bag on the floor by the door.

He hadn't noticed any of it.

He went straight for the sofa and flipped on the television. As he settled the tuner on an Atlanta Braves game, I stood there for a moment, frozen in disbelief. The whole scene felt eerily familiar, like I was watching Ed Couch in *Fried Green Tomatoes* plop down in his recliner while ignoring the woman who had spent all day cooking for him. At least I had thought better of the Saran Wrap dress idea.

Had you asked me a few years ago, I would've laughed at the idea of being called a "people pleaser." My rigid adherence to rules doesn't always lend itself to making others happy. Otherwise, I generally live under a "live and let live" credo, leaving others alone to live as they please unless they start hurting people, including themselves. That tends to mean the more I care about someone, the more uptight I may seem to them. Yet others have described me as laid-back, creating a dichotomy I've only recently begun to understand.

My own ranking on that scale tends to sit near the bottom, somewhere just north of "doormat." If I'm the only one being hurt, I'll allow someone every liberty they want to take until I simply can't shoulder it anymore. That tendency has led to more than a few outbursts over the years, which others may have perceived as irrational, unaware that the sudden loss of composure was the result of long-suppressed frustrations finally pouring out.

In a new relationship, it can take a long time for me to reach that threshold. In that moment, I simply couldn't bear to cause disruption, so…

I said nothing.

I blew out the candles, switched off the music, plated the lasagna, and handed him his food to eat on the sofa. Then I sat down at the table with the glass of wine I had poured for him, and ate the romantic dinner I had put so much thought into, alone.

From that night on, every time he came home from the road, he'd greet me by holding out a plastic grocery bag with a proud look on his face, and then he would go into the living room to watch TV. Inside the bag would be a frozen lasagna I was expected to make for dinner and a bottle of cheap wine. It may have been well-intentioned, but it still served as a reminder that I had tied myself to someone with no imagination who only put in the least amount of effort possible.

In spite of the growing difficulty of ignoring our mismatched personalities, ambitions, and education, I let my desperation for stability drown out reason, silencing the blaring sirens in my head.

In December 1997, nearly a year and a half after we met in that smoky country dance club, I agreed to marry him.

The fact that we had no friends to invite to a wedding needn't matter when we had no money to throw one. We bought simple dress clothes at a discount store and applied for a license. His grandfather, an ordained minister, would perform the ceremony at his home in Murfreesboro the following week.

As I applied my wedding day makeup in the spare bedroom of Gary's grandparents' home just before we took our vows, his grandmother barged in, shoved me aside from the mirror, and rummaged through a drawer in the vanity. She muttered dismissively, "Why are you doing that? It's just us." It was an act that seemed to set the tone for the marriage to follow.

Gary's parents, grandparents, aunt, and two cousins settled in the living room as if gathering for family movie night. I searched for some real acknowledgment of the occasion, but the only marker of any kind of special day was a small bowl of Jordan almonds that had appeared on the kitchen counter. I couldn't recall another time when something that should have mattered so much was treated as if it was barely happening.

While I was assembling myself, Jo Ann and my mother had arrived wearing their Sunday best, looking fully out of place among his family lounging apathetically in jeans and T-shirts, as if they had just rolled out of bed.

Afterward, we scrawled "Just Married" in shoe polish on the back window of my car and took off toward Atlanta with no plan and no reservations. After a few failed attempts, we finally found a budget hotel vacancy somewhere near Chattanooga. In an obvious attempt to score a free upgrade, we informed the desk clerk it was our wedding night. He offered a halfhearted "congratulations," and handed over the key to the only room with a Jacuzzi tub, mumbling about how they didn't have a honeymoon suite but this was "a special room, too."

Our "honeymoon" lasted exactly one night. The next morning, we packed up, checked out, and returned to normal life as if nothing had changed.

The wedding, or marriage as it were, played out against the backdrop of a pop culture phenomenon unlike anything our generation had seen. *Titanic* dominated the news, radio waves, and gossip columns for months leading up to and after the wedding. The movie's anthem, "My Heart Will Go On," became the accidental theme song of our wedding week. I had been anticipating this movie ever since my local movie theater put up a huge cardboard standee promoting it long before it was ever released, but all this "wedding nonsense" (as M'Lynn from *Steel Magnolias* might say) had delayed me in seeing it by several weeks.

Despite my aversion to crowds, Gary and I managed to squeeze into a packed theater in February 1998 for my first viewing of the long-awaited "big ship" movie. Up until that day, I had never seen a single film starring either of the lead actors. In hindsight, that may have heightened the emotional impact, allowing me to experience *Titanic* with no preconceived notions.

As I sat elbow-to-elbow with a stranger to my right, I had an overwhelming sense that I could not share the emotion of that moment with the stranger to my left, my new husband. Something told me he didn't have the capacity to understand the intensity I felt. As we left the theater, a cloud settled over me.

On the drive back to our little rental in North Knoxville from the theater, I sat in complete silence, watching the frigid world outside zip past the car windows, a world bustling with people unaware of the private devastation inside the vehicle. It felt as if I had just learned someone very close to me had died. I barely spoke a word the rest of the evening.

In the days and weeks that followed, I wondered if that lingering sorrow had set off a sudden, insatiable need to learn everything about the young, blonde-haired actor with striking aqua blue eyes that I'd never seen before. What started as curiosity soon escalated into an acute celebrity crush, what some might call limerence, shared by thousands of other girls and women the world over.

"Leomania" (a word play on the "Beatlemania" craze of the '60s) became almost as much of a phenomenon as the film itself, launching Leonardo DiCaprio into the stratosphere of stardom. His face was *everywhere*, saturating pop culture with every conceivable detail about his life and work.

The moment Gary was back on the road, I began collecting magazines filled with DiCaprio's photographs and renting every movie he had made up to that point. I kept a blank VHS tape at the ready, poised to record any fleeting glimpse of him in the entertainment segments on the news. I craved candid footage, anything that might offer a hint of what he was really like in person. When I discovered we were born the same year, it only deepened the surreal sense of kinship I felt to him, as if that small coincidence somehow justified the magnitude of my fixation.

What started as a powerful and slightly embarrassing celebrity crush speedily evolved into something far more significant. I was experiencing an awakening. With this new perspective, I could no longer ignore the truths I had spent the past year suppressing about my relationship.

Gary seemed to take my newfound obsession in stride. He never questioned the movie posters I hung in the spare bedroom of our apartment or even objected when I began sleeping in there even when he was home, blaming his snoring for my sudden inability to share the bed. To this day, I don't know if he ever suspected just how deep my feelings had become. What I do know is that he had no idea I had already lost all desire to be married to him and saw no future for us.

I finally accepted the truth I had been avoiding. I had married my husband out of fear alone. I was not attracted to him physically, emotionally, or intellectually. We had little in common, and for the first time, I was willing to admit that to myself. Finding the gumption to admit it to him would take almost another year.

Chapter 3: On the Street Where He Lives

"The callers can tell you're reading," Sharon scolded.

I laughed it off and promised to do better, but I had found myself in a choke-hold, struggling to feign interest in my work. Though there were few restrictions on our online activities, it was still a call center, and we were expected to at least sound engaged. Official Computer Use Agreements weren't a thing yet, mostly because management hadn't figured out what to do with our newfound internet access. In the summer of 1998, the Windows 95 computers had only just replaced the 20-year-old "dumb terminals" a few weeks before.

Aside from the woman five seats down who passive-aggressively commented on my perfume as I passed by her desk, Sharon was the only one who ever chastised me. My own supervisor, Dan, was usually too entertained by my brassy brand of customer service to care what I was doing, as long as I kept my calls under control. But today he was out of the office, leaving Sharon to take on the role of enforcer. And, to be fair, she had just cause to bark at me, except I wasn't "reading." I was *investigating.*

The first thing I searched for when I logged onto my new, internet-capable computer was news about my latest celebrity crush, Leonardo DiCaprio. Within seconds, I uncovered troves of trivia, photographs, and interviews. Online tabloid magazines churned out daily reports, tracking the newest superstar's every move with the tenacity of a mafia stake-out. A resourceful fan could easily find forums posting near real-time updates on his whereabouts, with users devotedly dissecting every sighting.

In interviews, he often spoke about refusing to let the constant attention turn him into a recluse, insisting that he wouldn't let fame keep him locked away. As a result, there was no shortage of tabloid fodder about a young, beautiful man-about-town who had swiftly become a fixture of the Los Angeles late-night celebrity hot spots.

This experience was in stark contrast to the last time I had a full-blown celebrity crush, back in the pre-internet days of 1987, when I was just 13. Having recently acquired my so-called "teen card," I wasted no time putting it to use, glomming onto one of the "Kids from *Fame*."

Billy Hufsey had been added to the cast of the *Fame* television series in 1983 as the resident heartthrob after the show moved to Fox, a network that, thanks to our rural location and rooftop antenna, had terrible reception especially on rainy days. When storm clouds rolled in on show day, I braced myself for heartbreak, secretly begging the universe not to rob me of my one connection to my latest obsession that week.

Both *Fame* the series and the 1980 movie it was based on were set in a fictional performing arts high school in New York City. It was the *Glee* of the '80s, with a large, multitalented cast. But for me, it was mostly about Billy. He danced and sang his way onto my bedroom walls, immortalized in glossy, nearly-naked posters. One of Tiger Beat Magazine's biggest controversies of the day was a now-infamous pinup of Billy wearing nothing but a thin, wet hand towel.

While that one made waves, I had my own favorite. The poster featured him standing in front of a deep red, textured backdrop, his amber eyes smoldering at the camera with the kind of come-hither stare that '80s heartthrobs were known for. His dark, curly mullet framed his face like a perfectly coiffed lion's mane, sitting just above the pièce de résistance: a black leather jacket with zebra-print fur trim, long leather fringe cascading across the back and down the sleeves, and absolutely nothing underneath to obscure his tanned, sculpted abs.

It was the epitome of '80s fashion, unapologetically gaudy, and to my early teenage eyes, irresistibly sexy.

This poster didn't just grace the wall above my bed, it went wherever I did. Since there weren't many other pictures of my amore available to me, I took matters into my own hands. I clipped a miniature version of the red poster from the mail-order pages of a magazine, cutting around the edges of the sample image like it was a priceless artifact.

To keep it from disintegrating from constant handling, I laminated it the best way a teenager could, by pressing strips of packing tape over it until it had a glossy, plastic-like sheen. It lived in my pink Jordache purse among the Carmex lip balm pots and hair barrettes, a treasured keepsake that I would sneak glances at throughout the day, until the unthinkable happened. A schoolmate caught sight of it, snatched it up, and mockingly teased me for carrying a picture of Patrick Swayze. *As if!*

My mother's sister had been making sincere efforts to forge a relationship with me through regular outings, including an escape to East Towne Mall. I seized the opportunity to add to my poster collection, making a beeline for Spencer's as soon as we walked through the doors. She didn't seem to mind the awkward trek to the risqué back section of the store where the poster display was located, even though it meant navigating past racks of black light posters, novelty handcuffs, and suggestively shaped drinking straws. What she *did* take issue with was the nature of the images I was there to purchase.

My mother was far less concerned with the posters themselves. She merely shrugged off my aunt's mild protests about the impropriety of covering my bedroom walls with images of a nearly naked man more than twice my age, reasoning that she didn't mind because he was 2,000 miles away.

The comment shattered me. Until that moment, in my barely teenage naiveté, I had truly believed he was in New York, a much more reasonable 650 miles from Tennessee. The idea that he was actually living across the country made him feel inconceivably far away, not that I would have gone even if I could. But still, 650 miles felt at least possible. Two *thousand* miles? That was another universe.

A decade later, I no longer had to rely on grainy television broadcasts, wrinkled magazine pages, or the fragile illusion that my latest crush was somehow within reach. Now, with the connectivity provided by my new work computer, Leo was just a click away.

Each morning brought a new batch of photos from the previous night's club escapades: Leo in a dimly lit VIP booth, Leo ducking into a waiting car, Leo hiding beneath the bill of a black baseball cap with a scantily clad young woman right behind. The endless supply of new content made life in the humdrum cube farm almost bearable.

Despite the lack of official rules about work-time internet browsing, I had an inkling that Sharon would disapprove of my cyberstalking activities anyway, especially once I stumbled upon the vast world of Leo fan pages. These sites were laboriously curated shrines, with photo albums filled to the brim with images their creators had clearly spent hours collecting and organizing. I picked out a handful of favorites that appeared to be updated regularly, trusting the site owners to provide me with all the daily Leo news.

A jealous *heeeeeeey, I want a page like this* brewed in the back of my mind, igniting a curiosity I couldn't shake. Eventually, I found myself researching how to create one of my own, and the rush of discovery took hold. It was the same childlike wonder I'd felt years before when I first figured out how to make that old TRS-80 do anything beyond play cartridge games.

I immediately discovered a handful of free homepage services, each promising an easy way to build a website with step-by-step wizards and a variety of templates. After some trial and error, I settled on GeoCities for its clean, easy-to-use interface and set to work crafting my very first website that I called "DiCaprio Street."

GeoCities categorized its homepages into "neighborhoods," each loosely themed around different interests. Naturally, I chose the Hollywood neighborhood for my Leo fan site. And if I was going to live in the Hollywood neighborhood, then of course my home had to be on DiCaprio Street. It seemed perfectly logical. Now, that lack of imagination makes me laugh at myself, especially since I had no way to create custom road-themed graphics to help the name make sense to new visitors. Then again, road-themed graphics wouldn't have made much sense on a Leonardo DiCaprio fan site either, so maybe it was for the best.

The first draft of my new website was embarrassingly simple: a plain burgundy expanse with the words "DiCaprio Street" in bold text above a single photograph of Leo, scavenged from another fan's site, centered on the page. The only interactive elements were an "Email Me" icon which linked to my brand-new Hotmail account created solely to sign up for GeoCities, and a guestbook for visitors to leave messages. There were no fancy layouts, no glittering animations, and no lists of partner fan sites, just the barest bones of what I hoped would eventually be a proper fan site.

I published the page and pushed my chair back from my cubicle, inspecting it from a distance like stepping away from a painting to see the full effect.

That'll do for now, I thought.

It was live, at least, but I wasn't about to stop there. I rolled up my metaphorical sleeves and dove into figuring out how to replicate all the flashy features I saw on every other fan page. Once I discovered the HTML code editor in GeoCities and realized I could use it to paste in my own code to customize the prebuilt site from the wizard, I was off to the races.

All I had to do was track down the code for the features I wanted and learn just enough HTML to fix the layout when my attempts to insert it inevitably broke the page. More often than not, a single misplaced tag would send everything spiraling into chaos, turning my methodically arranged site into an unrecognizable mess. But with each mistake, I learned a little more, and soon I was having more fun troubleshooting and polishing the site itself than adding content.

The next few weeks were a flurry of learning as I figured out how to add what is now considered classic '90s internet nostalgia. I proudly installed a hit counter that looked like an analog odometer to track page views, marquee text that scrolled welcome messages across the screen, and a visitor poll where fans could vote on the best Leo movie. Every day, I found new little tricks to make DiCaprio Street feel more refined, or at least more in line with what other fan pages were doing.

While I looked to other fan sites for inspiration, in those days many webmasters had no restraint when it came to embellishments. I loved experimenting with different features, but I found most animated GIFs of the day downright obnoxious and avoided them when I could. Others, however, seemed determined to be as irritating as possible, filling their pages with blinking text, seizure-inducing banners, and, worst of all, auto-play MIDI files of "My Heart Will Go On." This was especially problematic for those of us surfing the web from work, where the sudden blast of tinny pan flute could send a person scrambling for the mute button in embarrassment.

Of course, no fan site was complete without an overflowing photo gallery. I stuffed mine to the gills with every unique picture of Leo I could "borrow" from other fan pages, thoughtfully organizing them into themed albums. Cataloging those images instantly became my favorite between-call pastime, a welcome distraction from the drudgery of appliance parts ordering.

It wasn't long before this pastime earned me my first nastygram, the kind that really put the *Hot* in Hotmail. The owner of another fan site sent a scathing email demanding that I remove a picture I had scraped from her album, insisting she could tell it was her personal scan from a hardcopy magazine. I hastily obliged and took the photo down, though I couldn't help but roll my eyes. She had no real claim to it either. None of us did.

We were all blatantly violating copyright laws without a shred of shame, gleefully scanning and swapping images as if they belonged to us. Any reasonably intelligent fan site owner should have just accepted that we were all part of an unspoken, illegal photo exchange and moved on. But of course, people attempted to declare ownership anyway, as if they had exclusive rights to a mass-produced teen magazine clipping.

With all the prerequisite bells and whistles in place, I obsessively reloaded my page to accomplish two things. First, to put some digits on that hit counter as if that could hide the fact that it was a subpar fan site, and second, to check if there were any legitimate visits that I hadn't added myself. It became my first real taste of trying to hide the lack of engagement on content I've created, a humiliating little ritual I've had far too much practice with ever since.

Completely ignorant of how web traffic actually worked, I grew increasingly frustrated that all my hard work and self-taught HTML skills were being seen by exactly no one. I couldn't understand why my fan site wasn't racking up guestbook entries like all the others. If I had looked closer, I'd have realized those sites had been online collecting signatures for months. My impatience was getting the better of me, but I knew it was time for a little self-promotion.

Every self-respecting '90s fan page had one thing in common, no matter who it was dedicated to: *WebRing*. Once listed in a relevant directory, all you had to do was add the WebRing navigation bar to the bottom of your homepage, allowing visitors to seamlessly hop from one fan page to the next in an endless loop of admiration. It was the closest thing to a structured network that fan sites had in those early days of online fandoms, and getting listed felt like an initiation into the internet's inner circle of super-fans.

I threw myself into every promotional tactic I could find, but no matter how persistent I was, DiCaprio Street never seemed to gain any real traction. The hit counter ticked up at an excruciatingly slow pace, and I was lucky to get even one visitor a day. Each time I checked my guestbook, I was met with the same empty page. The lack of progress was maddening.

I was beginning to accept that the fandom was simply oversaturated. A few well-established sites that had launched before *Titanic* were thriving, drawing in steady traffic and supporting dedicated communities. Meanwhile, the countless fan pages that sprang up in the movie's wake were drowning in competition, struggling to carve out a space in an already overcrowded corner of the internet. After finally giving up hope, I abandoned DiCaprio Street to the virtual tumbleweeds, resigning myself to the fact that it would never be more than a tiny, unnoticed blip in the infinite sea of Leo devotion.

And then, purely by accident, I stumbled upon a very active but unobtrusive message board called "Leo's Sand Bar."

Leo's fans had been restlessly awaiting news of his first post-Titanic project when, in July 1998, it was announced he would star in *The Beach*, a role widely believed to be promised to Ewan McGregor. Ewan had never officially signed on, but the studio, eager to cash in on DiCaprio's meteoric fame, made a last-minute decision to hand him the part instead. Ewan's loss was our gain: we'd get to see Leo running around shirtless for his sacrifice.

Filming was set to begin in Thailand in January 1999, primarily on Ko Phi Phi Leh, a scenic island that would later be physically and digitally altered to better resemble the secluded tropical paradise described in the novel, complete with an enclosed lagoon. While fans waited for filming to begin, the Leo's Sand Bar (LSB) message board, housed on a larger parent website called "Sunrise by the Shore," was soaring in popularity thanks to fans looking for information about the area.

Sunrise by the Shore had been created as a class project by students at a primary school located about 430 miles north of the island, as a way to track the film's production. Their teacher, Richard Bradley, saw their proximity to the filming locations in Bangkok as an opportunity to give students hands-on experience in building and managing a website while also providing exclusive daily updates that no other fan sites could offer.

Riding the wave of *Titanic*-fueled Leomania, Sunrise by the Shore and its Leo's Sand Bar message board promptly became a hub for online fans craving any scrap of news about Leo's next big project. It became colloquially known as "The Thai Kids' Site," and everyone knew where to find it.

What neither the student webmasters nor the fans realized, at least not at first, was that they weren't the only ones who knew what people meant when someone mentioned the "Thai Kids."

Leo had learned that name, too.

Chapter 4: A Beach of Our Own

Around Thanksgiving of 1998, I learned that Dan had taken another job, leaving me without my only ally in management. Until further notice, Sharon would be supervising both teams.

I'm not sure if that revelation was the last straw or if my morale had already worn too thin, but my mornings soon fell into the same grim ritual. I would pull into the call center parking lot and sit there in silence, gripping the steering wheel with white-knuckled dread, scowling at the building as if it were sitting there, waiting to devour my life force the moment I swiped my badge. I'd wait until the last possible second before forcing myself inside, breezing past Sharon as she glanced down at her watch, only to find that I had beaten the clock by exactly one minute. *HA! No write-ups today!*

Anyone who has ever worked in a public-facing job knows the truth. They are only tolerable for about six months before the willful ignorance of certain customers and the slow grind of workplace politics start gnawing at your very soul. By December 1998, I had been there eight.

Customers frequently called the appliance call center while holding the answer to the question they called to ask right in their hot little hands. Instead of reading the owner's manual, they only used it to find the phone number. Knowing they preferred to call and have us look the information up for them rather than quickly flip through a few pages to find the answer themselves always had a slight demeaning bite to it, like a rude restaurant customer snapping their fingers to get a waiter's attention.

Beyond processing the less complicated parts orders, our section primarily existed to prescreen calls before forwarding more complicated issues to the parts specialist queue. We were the soldiers on the front line, sorting out the easy questions from the ones that required actual expertise. It was a thankless job, made worse by the realization that the people we transferred calls to, the ones we spared from arguing with stubborn customers over whether or not their ceiling fan was an appliance, were making a lot more than we were and had better digs besides.

For me, the introduction of the internet to our workplace was a double-edged sword. On one hand, it breathed life into an otherwise spirit-crushing job, giving me something, *anything*, to look forward to between calls. On the other hand, once I discovered the Leo's Sand Bar message board, the job itself became the unwelcome distraction.

Now the callers weren't just bothering me with their unnecessary questions, they were *interrupting* me. Every time the phone rang, it yanked me out of whatever thread I was immersed in, forcing me to shift gears from devouring Leo news to explaining yet again that

"I think 'whirlpool' is just the type of tub it is, sir, not the company that makes it."

After failing to get DiCaprio Street to grow any roots, LSB introduced me to something far more rewarding, though I wouldn't recognize it for what it was until years later. It was my first experience with engagement-driven dopamine hits.

Leo's Sand Bar was built on a free InsideTheWeb message board, one of many Richard Bradley added over time to the Sunrise by the Shore section of the Thai Kids' school website. For a new internetter like myself in 1998 and 1999, the LSB InsideTheWeb message board felt cutting-edge. A modern web surfer might compare it to a crude version of Reddit.

Each separate forum functioned like a subreddit, but instead of displaying just a list of subject lines, every new post appeared in full, often accompanied by large, full page photographs. Replies were listed directly beneath the original post, each one also appearing in full rather than collapsed behind a link. The resulting wall of text could tax even the most toned scrolling finger.

The members of LSB seemed to have already formed a tightknit community. After spending a few days observing their activity, I worked up the nerve to post my first message. It was a simple introduction, but making my first-ever public post on a forum had made me nervous.

Subject: New In Town

Hello everyone! I've been lurking a few days trying to get a feel for the board since I haven't been online very long. I've never even made a message board post like this before! I'm 24 (born the same year as Leo), from Tennessee. I found this site while looking for news about The Beach. Can't wait to get to know you all!

The replies I had hoped for and expected trickled in, warm welcomes all around. It was exactly the encouragement I needed. From there, it was just a matter of crafting posts that showed my personality and dry, sarcastic sense of humor. I often describe my humor as "Chandler Bing, but more awkward." I love a good one-liner, but my comedic timing is absolutely tragic.

It's funny how memory works. In my mind, LSB felt as fast-paced as a trending Twitter hashtag, with new posts flying by at breakneck speed. But in reality, it wasn't quite that busy. There was always someone online, ready to reply to new posts, that much was true, but it wasn't an overwhelming barrage of nonstop messages.

Maybe it was the anticipation that made it feel so alive. I knew a reply was coming, and the wait made every interaction feel more urgent. Between work calls, I would refresh the page several times a minute, my impatience distorting my memory and making it seem like more of a continuous stream than it really was.

Our crackpot team of LSB "investigators" worked with near-professional efficiency, manually scraping the newest photos of our anointed one from various entertainment news sites and posting them to the board almost as soon as they had been made public. Though I never had much interest in obsessively reloading tabloid sites waiting for a fresh story about Leo to appear, I couldn't help but feel a little jealous of the ladies who always seemed to have the jump on the rest of us. They made it look effortless, as if they had inside connections feeding them exclusives. I had to admire their commitment, even if I knew I'd never be part of their "breaking news crew."

The Beach hadn't even started filming yet and Leo's Sand Bar had already become one of the main online hot spots for fans. It was a place where no detail was too small, no photo too insignificant to be scrutinized. Of course, not everyone took our enthusiasm seriously. Naysayers would occasionally drop by just to mock the way we analyzed every new image and bit of news pixel by pixel.

"Look at the way his eyes look extra pale in this one."
"Do you see that vein in his forearm? *SWOON.*"
"You can tell by the way he's looking at that woman, they're sleeping together."

It was all in good fun, or so we thought.

The demographics of our ranks varied wildly, but they generally didn't include anyone under 18. Despite Leo's reputation for having a very young fan base, LSB had surprisingly few teenage members. His legions of younger fans were the ones who showed up at his events in hysterics, screaming and shaking uncontrollably at the slightest glance from him, as if they were looking at a god incarnate. By then, he was a staple on the covers of Tiger Beat and Teen People, his status as the reigning teen heartthrob fully cemented.

The user base of LSB skewed a bit older, perhaps because internet access was still relatively limited. Most families that did have access only had a single home computer to share. For younger fans, this meant competing for internet time with parents or siblings, making it more difficult to participate in online fandoms as easily as older women who had more control over their screen time. As a result, the most active users on LSB weren't the screaming teenyboppers Leo was used to seeing in public, but a mix of young adults and older fans who approached their obsession in a more mature way, even if only slightly more so.

At 24, I was one of the younger LSB regulars, but age didn't seem to matter much in the grand scheme of things. Several women well over 50 posted just as fervently as the rest of us, drooling over every new photo and examining his latest interviews for any small glimpse into his private world. In the days of Leomania, it didn't strike me as unusual. We were all just fans, united in our collective admiration.

Looking back as a now-50-plus woman myself, I'm not sure I see the same appeal. These days, 24-year-old men barely register on my radar, so I can't imagine having the same reaction to Leo if I'd been twice his age back then. Maybe it was the *Titanic* effect, that perfect storm of talent, charisma, and Hollywood's relentless push to market him as the ultimate heartthrob. Or maybe some of the older women were simply caught up in the fun of it all, indulging in the fantasy without taking it too seriously.

Either way, nobody questioned it. Leo belonged to all of us and none of us equally.

Nonetheless, the replies to the daily photo drops grew increasingly... *interesting*. What started as innocent fascination soon took a turn, evolving from playful commentary to more detailed discussions about certain preferences and habits.

Soon, those same images became visual aids for fan fiction, serving as inspiration for elaborate stories that went well beyond harmless celebrity crushes. What had begun as a simple message board for news and gossip had slowly transformed into something much more imaginative. Most stories were romantic, many pushing the boundaries into heavily suggestive territory. Some were sensational, and some… well, some were just oddly specific.

I vividly remember the one that started it all. One of the less vocal regulars posted something that was less a story and more like a description of a painting. It perfectly captured an almost picturesque scene of Leo sitting cross-legged on the floor, clipping his toenails. That was it. No grand romance, no intense narrative. Just Leo, a pair of nail clippers, and an unexpectedly intimate glimpse into his personal hygiene routine.

In hindsight, it was a peculiar creative choice. But at the time? It seemed like a perfectly reasonable thing for a mature fan to imagine. Just a simple, ordinary moment in the life of a normal, albeit very famous, young man. If anything, it was almost refreshing. It was a reminder that beyond the reach of the Hollywood lights, even the most celebrated among us is still only human.

Somewhere along the line, we all seemed to have forgotten who was running this site. What had started as a harmless gathering of devoted fans had begun to edge slightly beyond PG-13, a smidge too spicy for a website that, after all, was run by schoolchildren.

We began to acknowledge that maybe we had outgrown LSB, at least for this type of content. LSB would always be a home base for news and photographs, but we needed a more appropriate place for our fan fiction.

[Cracks knuckles]

I got this.

Chapter 5: An Island in Choppy Seas

I almost don't remember what it was like not having a screen in front of my face every minute of the day. Several times a day, I'll catch myself checking email on my phone while scrolling through social media on a tablet, with a TV or computer humming in the background. Over the years I've developed the attention span of a goldfish and a robust connectivity addiction.

In 1998, not only did I not have a cell phone or tablet, I didn't even have a computer at home. If I wanted to build websites, I had to do it at work, and that meant no image editing programs or fancy design tools. Fortunately, the internet was full of workarounds. Industrious programmers had created free image generators, and repositories were overflowing with background graphics, coordinating navigation buttons, and an endless supply of animated GIFs.

I spent hours paging through the graphics libraries, painstakingly selecting the perfect suite of images for a brand-new website. This time, I already had a user base clamoring for a fan site where their fan fiction would be welcome. I named it "Paradise Island."

Once again, I can't say I was particularly proud of my lack of imagination when it came to naming websites, but I didn't let that get in my way. The name fit well enough, and I had bigger things to worry about, like making sure it looked *just* right. For the background, I selected a tiled image in shades of pink and burgundy with a marbled ink pattern, completely ignoring the more obvious choice of blue to suggest water. Modern web surfers would find it obnoxious and distracting, but it gave the homepage a rich, luxurious feel by comparison to other late '90s fan sites covered in flashing banners and GIFs. Or at least, that's what I told myself as I eagerly pieced it all together.

Centered on the page was a posed photograph of Leo from the January 1998 issue of Vanity Fair, one I had specifically selected for its effortless fusion of sophistication and just the right amount of tease. He was lounging on an outdoor platform propped up on his elbow, his white long-sleeved button-down shirt paired with a black vest, left untucked and open at the bottom just enough to reveal a hint of his belly button. The outfit was finished off with slim black pants and snakeskin loafers to give the look an air of elegance that perfectly fit the vibe I was going for.

Beneath the photo were four navigation buttons I had created using an online graphics generator. It allowed me to "buttonize" my background tile, transforming it into coordinating square buttons with a drop shadow and overlaid text. The features they linked to were typical of most fan pages that struggled to find relevant content: Message Board, About Us, Photos, and Contact Us. It was all coming together, and for the first time, I had something that felt like a real website, something that could compete with even the most popular of fan sites.

From my time lurking on the Leo's Sand Bar message board, I knew one thing for certain. If Paradise Island was going to thrive, we would need a team of moderators. The board needed people who could monitor discussions around the clock, ready to step in and remove anything that got a little too steamy for prime time.

I strategically assembled a small team from different time zones, choosing moderators I could trust to handle the task with some level of discretion. To give the site a sense of structure, I added a short blurb about each of them on the About Us page, introducing them as the peacekeepers of our growing community. Having a whole team of women behind Paradise Island gave the site an added layer of legitimacy. I wanted it to feel like an established fan hub rather than just another amateurish fan page destined to fade into obscurity.

We were up and running in just a couple of days. With Richard's blessing, I posted the link on the LSB message board, directing the regulars who had been engaging with fanfic posts there to the new site. The response was immediate.

At last, I had the popular site I had been craving, but without the exhausting hours of promotion or the need to clutter the homepage with banner exchanges and WebRing navigators. Paradise Island practically advertised itself. The new message board buzzed with activity, nearly as busy as LSB, with new posts rolling in day and night.

I was a proud web mama.

Back in the real world, Brad, the 20-year-old in the cube next door, had caught on to my side project and wasted no time launching into a full-blown teasing fury. The fact that I had built another Leo website was entertaining enough for him, but what really sent him over the edge was the fan fiction. He cackled as he labeled it "soft porn."

He was more amused than anything, but his raucous laughter had an unintended consequence. I suspect it inadvertently tipped off Sharon, whose disapproval of me only seemed to deepen by the day. The last thing I needed was to give her any more excuses to target me for disciplinary action.

I knew that keeping Paradise Island active meant engaging as much as possible with each new post. It would require encouraging writers, welcoming newcomers, and trying to coax lurking visitors out of the shadows. The moderators were always around, but as the site's owner, I felt duty-bound to be the head cheerleader. I wanted to ensure each new post had multiple positive replies to make participating feel worthwhile. I'd simply have to find a way to manage the website off the clock.

The only problem was, I couldn't afford a computer.

Luckily for me, the Philips-Magnavox Outlet at the Red Roof Mall was just up the road in Pigeon Forge, Tennessee. Among their offerings was a device that seemed like the perfect solution: a WebTV console. It was a small box that connected to a television and provided dial-up internet access, controlled through either a remote control or a wireless keyboard.

For less than $130, plus a $20-per-month dial-up subscription fee, I was back in business. Or at least, mostly back in business.

Without a mouse to point and click through links, WebTV's interface was unwieldy at best. Navigation relied on paging through clickable links, similar to how you might use the Tab key to highlight elements on a computer when the mouse stops working. It was far from ideal, but considering my only other option was managing Paradise Island exclusively from the office, I was more than willing to make it work.

The biggest challenge was WebTV's lack of an internal hard drive. Without one, I couldn't download anything, including the graphics I had been creating with online generators. That was a major setback. My ability to customize Paradise Island relied on those images, and without a way to save and upload them, my site would be stuck in its current state.

Determined to find a workaround, I began researching and discovered a small collective of WebTV users who had already solved this exact problem. Several services catered specifically to WebTV webmasters, allowing users to create graphics and save them directly to their GeoCities storage. It wasn't as seamless as working on a real computer, but it was good enough to keep Paradise Island running, and that was all that mattered.

Was it ideal? No. Did it work? Yes. Is the little *gopuck* noise the navigation made still ingrained in my head more than two and a half decades later? Also yes.

It wasn't until a few days after setting up the WebTV box that I realized something. I had never mentioned any of this to Gary. The thought hit me when he called to say he was on his way home from the road, and all of a sudden, the little black console now on display in our living room felt a lot more conspicuous.

In those days, $130 was a big purchase for our little family, and I probably should have waited to discuss it with him. But the deed was done and there it sat, already gathering dust on the particleboard entertainment center I had brought from my parents' house when we moved in together. There was no hiding it now.

When he arrived, I did my best to explain why I needed it without sounding like an obsessive nut job. I walked him through how it worked, expecting at least some level of curiosity. Instead, I discovered a much bigger issue.

He didn't even comprehend what the internet was.

I tried everything to make it click, describing the World Wide Web as a giant spider web of interconnected computers, each functioning like a series of spoke hubs. I broke it down in the simplest terms, explaining that anyone could build a website and that most businesses, government bodies, and just about any official entity had one. He furrowed his brow, deep in thought.

Finally, after a long pause, he asked, "Do the Braves have one?"

Hello, Face, have you met my friend, Palm?

That's a conversation I'm still rubbing my temples over more than 25 years later. If nothing else, it marked an important milestone in our relationship. It was the moment I realized with absolute certainty that we would never be on the same page about anything.

It only just occurred to me while writing this memoir that what happened next may have been retaliation for my unapproved purchase of the WebTV console, because soon after, Gary came home from the road driving a new pickup truck.

Maybe he figured that if we could afford WebTV, we could afford another car payment. Or maybe, in his mind, my purchase had granted him permission to buy himself a gift. Either way, although I handled our joint finances, he went ahead and made the deal without checking in with me. On his way home from dropping off his rig, he had his father cosign for the loan, sealing the purchase before I even knew he was considering it.

My father-in-law, Gary Sr., was a small-statured man with old military-issue "birth control glasses" and a full head of unkempt salt-and-pepper hair. His uniform never changed: jeans, scuffed brown work boots, and an ill-fitting short-sleeved button-down, its left breast pocket perpetually stocked with a pen and a spiral notepad.

What he lacked in size, he made up for in volume. He was boisterous, highly opinionated, and had a habit of barking orders like he expected the world to fall in line. Gary's shy, soft-spoken mother bore the brunt of it, enduring his father's forceful commands without complaint, a dynamic that made every visit just a little more uncomfortable. His grandparents weren't much better, abrasive and exhausting in their own ways.

I found myself dreading any time spent with any of them.

It had become clear that Gary didn't see me as his family. His father was his primary advisor, the one he turned to for every major decision, often without even asking for my input. No matter how much I tried to reason with him, his father's advice always seemed to carry more weight than mine. To make matters worse, he had an almost unhealthy attachment to his grandparents, as if their approval mattered more than building a future with his wife.

Shortly after Gary and I moved in together, his parents moved into a trailer set up on his grandfather's property in the outskirts of Murfreesboro. To my dismay, Gary envied that arrangement and dreamed of doing the same one day. To him, that was the ideal life, settling down in a double-wide in the country, surrounded by his parents and grandparents, living out some version of a rural family compound.

To me, that was an insurmountable difference in ambition. Growing up, I'd seen Georgian or Colonial-style houses in movies like *Home Alone*, *Meet the Parents*, and *Father of the Bride* portrayed as the quintessential middle-class American home. Those two-story white houses with symmetrical windows and a staircase right up the center felt like the mark of success, especially when nestled in neatly groomed neighborhoods where kids played in the street and neighbors waved as they walked their dogs down the sidewalks.

I've discovered a need for more separation from people in my later years, but as a young adult who'd spent their childhood in the isolation of the country, I yearned for the white-picket-fence American Dream. The idea of trading that for a trailer in the woods, parked next door to Gary's insufferable father and grandparents, wasn't just unappealing. It was incomprehensible.

Something about his father had always put me on edge. His vociferous, relentlessly negative opinions were steeped in a kind of stubbornness I'd grown used to among Tennessee country folk, but there was something nefarious lurking beneath the surface. My intuition had been sending up warning signals since our first meeting, whispering that there was a dirty underbelly I hadn't discovered. At least, not yet. Not until our wedding night.

As we soaked in the Jacuzzi tub of our budget hotel room the night of our wedding, Gary decided it was the perfect moment to divulge a secret he had been keeping. He admitted he had hidden it from me out of fear that I would judge him and now that the marriage contract was signed, he felt free to bring out the skeleton.

His father had a criminal record.

He had defrauded his own employer, embezzling $50,000 through falsified expense reports. More recently, he had packed up and moved back to Murfreesboro overnight, fleeing Kingston just before our wedding to dodge law enforcement over check fraud. That, as it turned out, was the real reason he was living on his father's property rather than in a house rented in his own name.

Yet, despite all of that, Gary still trusted him and accepted his financial advice without question. He even allowed him to prepare his tax return the previous year, as if a man with a prior fraud conviction was the most qualified person to handle accounting paperwork.

As I sat there, the bubbles from the Jacuzzi swirling around us, the implications of what he had just said settled over me. This wasn't just about having a father-in-law I didn't like. I was now chained to a man whose loyalty lay with someone who had already proven to be untrustworthy. And no matter how clearly I saw the problem, Gary refused to see it at all.

That tax return ended up instigating the first and last real argument we ever had.

In December of 1998, shortly after Paradise Island launched and just two weeks before Christmas, we received a notice that Gary's entire paycheck had been garnished by the IRS. No warning, no gradual deductions, just gone.

When his father prepared his tax return, he had padded it with a laundry list of false deductions, so many that the red flags practically waved themselves. Gary happily accepted the inflated refund not realizing it had been automatically processed, fully believing it must have been reviewed and deemed legitimate by an IRS worker before the money was released to our bank account. Months later, when the red flags finally brought it up for manual review, the IRS rescinded the refund and came to collect.

In an instant, Gary's paycheck vanished, at the worst possible time of year.

I never asked for much in general. In fact, I refused to be seen as a nag. I didn't spend money on clothes, never visited a salon, and rarely spent money on myself. Even the WebTV purchase had felt more like a necessity than a splurge. But Christmas was something I held sacred. This year, there would be nothing to celebrate.

In a moment of unadulterated frustration, I shelved my usual non-confrontational nature and yelled, "Who thinks they can actually claim all that crap?!"

Without missing a beat, Gary snapped back, "Do you think you're *better* than me?"

The question caught me off guard. It wasn't what I expected, not even close. I hadn't even been certain he could process information that rapidly before. I hesitated for half a second before sheepishly replying with a simple, "No," and walking away. But I couldn't outrun the sickening realization that I had, somehow, accidentally married into a family of fraudsters. And if I was being honest? Yeah, maybe I did think so, a little bit.

I waited until the holiday season was over. Then, the next time Gary came home from his latest over-the-road trip, I braced myself.

That last morning, I sat on the edge of the bed in the spare room with my *Titanic* poster still on the wall behind me, waiting. I knew he would come in to say good morning. When he did, he stood at the foot of the bed, expecting the usual routine.

Instead, I sat up, looked him directly in the face, and softly said, "I don't love you."

That was the last time I ever saw him.

Chapter 6: Batten Down the Hatches

"My husband left. I won't be able to pay the rent by myself, so I'm going to have to move out," I told my landlord when he stopped by for maintenance.

It wasn't a lie. He had left. A little omission to stir up a bit of sympathy never hurt when breaking a lease. He didn't need to know I was the one who ended it. If he pictured me as the jilted wife, abandoned by some cheating scoundrel, all the better.

He nodded solemnly, assured me he understood, and let me out of the lease without penalty. "Well, that sort of thing just can't be helped," he replied.

Gary gathered a few things and left as soon as I told him it was over, heading straight to his parents' place. A few days later, while I was at work, he came back and cleared out the rest of what he'd brought when we moved in together. I came home to find the bed from the primary bedroom, the washer and dryer, and the rest of his personal effects gone.

What I hadn't anticipated was that he'd also stopped by my mother's house to collect a small lawn mower we'd stored in the barn there. I hadn't warned her. I hadn't even told her about the breakup yet. His showing up in her driveway unannounced with his father in tow was the first she'd heard of any trouble between us.

Well, she knew now, and she made sure to tell me it was expected.

She and Jo Ann had apparently been baffled by my decision to marry someone so obviously ill-suited to me but had kept their opinions to themselves. They had watched, likely exchanging wary glances behind my back, as I signed myself up for a life they knew wouldn't fit. Not that it would have changed anything had they protested the match. If they had spoken up, it probably would have only made me dig in my heels deeper out of pure defiance.

In hindsight, I should've waited to break up until after the rent check that had already been mailed cleared, but hindsight wasn't going to pay my landlord. My soon-to-be ex-husband stopped his direct deposit immediately, the rent check bounced, and our already thin account plunged into the negative. It left me with nothing but the five dollars in my pocket to last two weeks until my next paycheck.

I scrambled to find friends and family who could help me move for free, knowing I had no choice but to pack up and, once again, return home. It wasn't a step forward, but at least it was a step out. Moving back home was the last thing I wanted, but it was far better than languishing in a loveless marriage. It felt like undoing all the progress I had made establishing myself as an adult, however flimsy that progress might have been at the ripe old age of 24.

Jo Ann was still living at home, only now with a rambunctious three-year-old whose default setting was "anarchy." Any hope for peace and quiet was already out the window. She also still had her computer, which meant I would be competing for precious phone line time to get on dial-up, a battle I wasn't sure I could win. On top of that, the move would double my already painful commute to the call center, which only served to make this whole arrangement feel even more like a punishment. It would be a tough pill to swallow but I was out of options.

As I begrudgingly packed my things, Brenda, a close friend who had already saved my hide by lending me money for food and gas, offered me a lifeline. She knew I was dreading the move back home, and as luck would have it, she had a connection that might keep me from taking that step backward.

The morning my uncle and cousins were scheduled to come pick up my things, Brenda took me to talk to her grandmother, who just so happened to own the small apartment complex where Brenda lived. It was a long shot, but at this point, I was willing to try anything.

Time to dust off the ol' jilted wife routine again. At this rate, I was practically ready for an Oscar.

Brenda explained how I'd been tragically left high and dry with nowhere to go and no money in the bank. Her grandmother needn't be told that I had my mother's house as an option. For all intents and purposes, neither one of us considered it one.

"I'll let you move in without a deposit, and you can just pay the first month's rent whenever you get it," her grandmother offered, barely giving it a second thought. As if that wasn't generous enough, she even agreed to a reduced monthly rate if I took one of the two upstairs units. She became my unexpected guardian angel, helping everything to fall into place exactly when I needed it most. I wasn't going to have to start over from my childhood bedroom after all.

The apartment was a small, two-bedroom, one-bath unit at the top of the stairs in a fourplex around the corner from Brenda's apartment building. It was smaller than the place I shared with Gary, but it was the perfect size for me and my new, scaled-back life.

Directly below me lived an elderly man I only knew as "Mr. Roberts." I would soon learn two things about him. One, he was hard of hearing and kept his TV blasting loud enough to be heard through the floor. Two, he still managed to hear every bit of noise I made, relentlessly complaining to the landlord each time I dared turn my own television up beyond a murmur.

I also discovered why the grandmother wasn't urgent about being paid. The property was barely maintained. My dishwasher didn't work, the foundation was infested with ants that made their way into the apartments, and the landscaping was left to rot. Tending to the flowerbeds in front of our fourplex became Mr. Roberts' primary retirement activity.

More often than not, though, he seemed less interested in gardening and more content to simply stand there, staring at the flowerbeds like they held the secrets of an afterlife he'd surely soon learn firsthand. This made sneaking past him to get upstairs a challenge, especially for a small-talk-averse new divorcée who just wanted to slip inside unnoticed, though the neighbor's son ensured that rarely happened.

The neighbor's boy was a teenager who lived in the unit beneath the vacant apartment next to mine with his parents. Their front door faced the base of the stairs that led up to mine, which became a bit awkward after they installed a glass storm door and started leaving the main door open at all hours. Their son spent most of his spare time standing directly behind the glass, watching the parking lot like a sentry and making unbroken eye contact as I descended the stairs each time I left.

I never met them, at least not formally, but their son reported my every move to Mr. Roberts in daily meetings by the flowerbed as if I were under house arrest, loudly delivering a running inventory of every item he saw coming into or leaving my apartment.

It never mattered. *None* of it mattered. With all its faults, the little apartment would soon be a beloved home.

When my uncle and cousins arrived to pick up what was left of me and my marriage, I met them at the door with a proud announcement. "There's been a change in destination," I declared, unable to hide the small spark of triumph in my voice. "We're not going to my mother's house."

I settled into my cheap little apartment and new life with absolute joy. At long last, I could unclench without the heaviness of suppressing myself. No more fantasizing about being single only to have the illusion intruded upon every two weeks by someone I spent the rest of the time daydreaming out of existence. No more pretending I was happy or faking gratitude for being tasked, yet again, with cooking a frozen lasagna as a poor imitation of my carefully planned romantic dinner date.

Every waking hour outside of work was spent logged into Paradise Island, cultivating a user base, fine-tuning this or that, and becoming consumed by my new online world.

At work, life at the call center stayed relatively unchanged, with the same stubborn customers, the same exhausting routine, and the same barely-veiled resentment brewing under the surface. That is, until one day, about a month after the move, in late February 1999.

Nothing of note had happened recently, but I was just as disenchanted with the job as ever. The days blurred together in an oppressive cycle of pointless calls and passive discontent, each shift feeling longer than the last. Then, on one otherwise unremarkable day, I went to the supervisor block to discuss something with Sharon. I was still standing there when a newer employee approached and asked her a question.

I don't know what came over me. Perhaps it was a dutiful urge to be helpful or maybe sheer muscle memory, but before Sharon could answer, I interjected and responded for her. It was only a simple clarification, a mundane technical detail, but the moment the words left my mouth, I knew I had made a mistake.

Sharon said nothing.

There was no nod of agreement, no acknowledgment, not even a glance of mild irritation.

The other employee and I returned to our desks without another word, finishing out the day as if nothing had happened. But something had. I just didn't realize it yet.

When I got home that evening, there was a message waiting on my answering machine. The temp agency, delivering the news in their usual detached tone, informed me that I was no longer needed at the call center. Nearly a year on the job. Never written up. Never saw anyone else get dismissed. And yet, I had finally rubbed Sharon the wrong way one time too many.

I find it funny looking back, because I don't remember this as a firing. To me, it felt more like a layoff. At least when I lost my job at the finance company, they had my being late one day due to traffic as an excuse. Here, they had no reason to let me go other than a personality clash.

I urgently called Stacey to let her know I wouldn't be able to get back into the building to grab my things. I asked if she could collect them for me and meet somewhere to hand them off. I wasn't too concerned about the desk toys or random promotional junk. I could live without those, but that *Titanic* ticket stub pinned to my cubicle wall? That was personal. It was a small but cherished keepsake from a night that had unknowingly set so much in motion.

Stacey was just as shocked as I was to hear I had been dismissed, though neither of us really questioned why. We both knew exactly whose fingerprints were all over it. Unfortunately, I never managed to meet up with her. My desk was emptied, my things packed into a box that would eventually be discarded, and the stub, the one thing I truly wanted back, was lost forever.

And now, I was jobless, living alone in a new apartment with no way to make good on my promise to catch the rent up.

I reluctantly picked up the phone and called my landlord, dreading the conversation. Fully expecting her to ask me to leave immediately, I braced myself for the worst. After all, I hadn't even paid the first month's rent yet. I was still struggling to recover from the financial gut punch of the breakup.

Instead of eviction notices or ultimatums, she simply said, "Just pay it whenever you can." No pressure, no lectures, no threats. It was the second time in as many months that this woman had bailed me out of a crisis, rescuing me from failing to launch, yet again.

I hung up the phone, feeling an overwhelming wave of relief crash over me. Now, I had work to do.

Monster.com was the gold standard for online job listings, but in early 1999, the Sunday newspaper was still the traditional go-to for finding employment. No matter how much the internet was expanding, old habits die hard, and dedicated job-seekers still turned to the classified ads first.

Newspaper delivery subscriptions came in a few flavors, one being Sunday only. Sunday was the one day of the week the newspaper came out in its full form, easily three to four inches thick, stuffed with ads, coupon flyers, oversized comics pages, and, most importantly, the supersized classifieds section. I only picked up my copies from the corner grocery whenever I had need for one, and job searching was usually that need. It was an event, a ritual for the unemployed.

Experienced job-seekers knew the drill: they grabbed the paper, spread it out on the kitchen table, and started circling anything that looked promising. Then, first thing Monday morning, the phone calls began, one after another, as they worked through the listings and hoped to catch someone before their inbox filled with too many résumés. If you were looking for retail work, you laced up your walking shoes and headed to the mall, stopping in every store to ask for an application. Within five years, this entire process would be replaced by online job boards.

And so, my new form of employment became keeping an eye on both the online and print ads, scouring, circling, and calling, while spending the rest of my time on Paradise Island. If nothing else, at least one of those things felt productive.

I let the Paradise Island moderators know what was going on with me, and they seemed appropriately horrified on my behalf. Their sympathy was comforting, but scaling back my activity was never an option. The site was the only constant in a life that had otherwise been turned completely upside down. I immersed myself in the forum, crafting new stories and engaging with other authors, finding solace in the steady rhythm of writing and conversation. It was an escape, a distraction, and, in many ways, the only thing keeping me from losing it.

Naturally a night owl, my hours of operation slipped later and later as the days of unemployment bled into weeks. Midnight turned into one, then two, until my schedule barely resembled anything normal. One Saturday night, I was online until at least two in the morning before sleepily toddling off to bed, completely unaware of what was about to unfold.

The next morning, I had barely managed to wipe the sleep from my eyes before I logged into Paradise Island to check for new posts from overnight, just as I always did… but something was off.

There was nothing new. Not a single new post was made after I logged off the night before. Not even a stray comment on an existing thread. It was eerily quiet.

Assuming something was wrong with the message board, I feverishly checked the InsideTheWeb website for outage notices, but there was no sign of trouble. I refreshed Paradise Island again. Still nothing new. Growing uneasy, I posted a casual "Is anyone alive out there?" message on the board, expecting at least someone to chime in.

Silence.

Just as I was about to fire off a support request to see if there was a technical issue, an email popped into my inbox.

"I felt bad watching you wonder what happened. I can't believe they couldn't at least tell you," one of the now-*former* Paradise Island regulars wrote.

I must have blocked out the rest of the email from memory. Even now, just thinking about it makes my chest tighten, the trauma of that moment still raw despite the years.

She laid it all out. The moderators I had trusted, the people I had chosen, had decided they didn't like how I'd been behaving. But when it came to what, exactly, had been so offensive, she was cryptic. She provided no specifics and no examples, just vague allusions to grievances they never had the decency to bring to me directly.

Instead of acknowledging that I was already going through a difficult time and simply talking to me, they had plotted behind my back. They had conspired to abandon Paradise Island and recreate it under a new name, "Paradise Isle."

They built their own GeoCities page, blatantly ripping off my design. They swapped in a blue version of the same marbled ink background tile I had so lovingly chosen, as if that minor tweak made it unique. They even used the same Vanity Fair photo of Leo that I had picked as the centerpiece of the homepage, like a trophy stolen in the night by a rival team.

But the real kicker? They set up a new InsideTheWeb message board with one crucial difference. This one required a pre-approved login, locking me out entirely.

They didn't stop there.

They coordinated with the regulars, made sure everyone had logins in advance, and then waited, calm and calculated, watching the clock. The moment I finally logged off in the early hours of Sunday morning, they made their move.

That's when they migrated everyone over, vanishing en masse and leaving me behind on what had once been my cherished, thriving message board.

Just me, the ghosts of old conversations, and the desolate echo of my own typing.

Chapter 7: A Plank-Walker's Petulance

It's been 84 years… well, actually just over 25, and I still don't have a single answer about what caused the Paradise Island moderators to stage a mutiny. I had never experienced an orchestrated backstabbing like it, and mercifully haven't since. One moment, everything was normal. The site was thriving, the message board was teeming with activity, and I was juggling posts, comments, and the usual day-to-day upkeep. The next, it had evaporated in a digital mushroom cloud, a nuclear blast detonated by my own friends.

In the aftermath, I racked my brain, scrolling through recent posts on the now-lifeless message board, grasping for any clue, any misstep, any seemingly innocent comment that might have been misinterpreted, something that could explain what I had done to deserve it. But no matter how many times I reread the threads, no matter how many angles I examined, the answer refused to reveal itself. What had I said? What had I done? It was a manic, all-consuming need for closure.

I was forced to accept blame without so much as the courtesy of being told what the crime had been. In the moment, I could only presume that the stress of the breakup, the sudden move, and then immediately losing my job had weighed on me more heavily than I realized, seeping unknowingly into my interactions on the board. Perhaps my usual sarcasm had twisted into something more unintentionally. biting, or my attempts at keeping things upbeat had come across as disingenuous. Or maybe, in my relentless push to reply to every new post and keep the board looking active, I had started to seem demanding, expecting too much from what should have been a lighthearted pastime.

But even if any or all of that had been true, was that really enough to justify what they did? I would have expected this kind of exile for someone who had done real harm, someone who had lashed out, become abusive, or made the space unsafe for others. Not *me.* I wasn't cruel. I hadn't harassed or berated anyone. Surely, they hadn't gone to these lengths just because they found me irritating… *had they*?

Looking back now, their reaction, whatever it was in response to, feels even more unreasonable and bizarre than it did at the time, especially coming from grown women. Time has only magnified just how drastic and unnecessary their actions were. When I consider that I later went on to be openly and exuberantly accepted by others in the LSB community, this event truly leaves me baffled.

I still occasionally wonder how long they had been plotting. How long had it taken to replicate my site? How had they managed to spread the word to all the regulars without tipping me off, and convince them all to go along with the blindside? I will never not be astonished by that.

It wasn't just a falling out. It was an overt betrayal, not just by the moderators I had personally chosen and trusted, but by every single regular who had gone along with their plan. These were people I had laughed with, shared stories with, and spent countless hours engaging with as if they were real friends. And yet, not one of them had the courage or compassion to warn me in advance, to pull me aside, or to even hint that something was coming. They had all watched me log in the next morning, alone and confused. It was only afterward that one of them finally felt bad enough to tell me what went down.

I mourned this more than my divorce. That loss had been inevitable, a slow unraveling I had seen coming for months. But this? This felt like the ground had split open and swallowed everything I thought was real. Paradise Island had been my refuge, my last tether to a sense of purpose after losing my job. It was the one thing keeping me connected, keeping me engaged, giving me something to focus on when everything else in my life had crumbled.

In a last ditch attempt to salvage what was left of my pride after the coup, I hurriedly archived the Paradise Island message board and pulled down the homepage. In its place, I slapped up a bizarrely space-themed fan page called "To the Stars," the kind of irrelevant concept based on the type of obscure reference I'd already written off back when DiCaprio Street failed. It wasn't meant to be serious.

It was just a placeholder that made it look like I had already moved on.

I even added a new, empty message board, just in case someone wandered by looking to reconnect. Maybe a few regulars hadn't been in on the plan. Maybe someone would see what happened and take my side. But when a lone supporter finally posted, clearly just feeling sorry for me, I realized how pathetic it all was. I took the board down immediately. Seeing that single, awkward message sitting there, a vain attempt at encouragement, made the humiliation feel even more searing.

I spent an entire day buried in my pillow, crying so intensely my chest ached and my face swelled. I lay in bed and sobbed until the sun faded away, and when shock finally gave way to resignation, the resulting depression pulled me into a deep, dreamless sleep.

When I awoke the next morning, the previous day's despair had morphed into something much darker. The heartbreak had boiled over into pure, undiluted rage. That's when I started to go off the rails in ways I'm still ashamed of.

I summoned Brenda for backup. She charged up to my apartment like a one-woman emergency response unit, ready to triage my emotional injuries and help me take strategic aim.

"This isn't an overreaction. This is justice," Brenda declared as we carefully crafted a complaint to InsideTheWeb.

"There is a website hosted on your service that is breaking your terms of service by posting adult-themed material," the email read. It was petty, I know, a classic *fine, if I can't have it, neither can you,* moment, but after everything, it felt cathartic in a way nothing else had. Besides, what harm could it really do? At worst, the site would be taken down, forcing them to start over.

And honestly? That felt like a fair consequence. They hadn't just abandoned me. They had stolen my entire design, right down to the layout and background. If they had built their own site from scratch and earned their traffic through legitimate competition, maybe I could've swallowed the betrayal. But they didn't. They took what I built, rebranded it, and locked me out. If reporting them meant they had to put in the same amount of effort I had, so be it.

As I sat back and waited for the new Paradise Isle site to sink, another email arrived.

"They know it was you who reported them," wrote the same former regular who had tipped me off about the coup.

My stomach dropped.

InsideTheWeb hadn't removed the site. They hadn't even issued a warning. Instead, they had forwarded my entire email to the coup's ringleader. To make matters worse, the forwarded message still contained the email header information, including my IP address, which pointed straight back to my location in Tennessee.

And of course, everyone knew I was the only Tennessean on Paradise Island.

Even as my face flushed with the realization that I had been caught, I refused to apologize. They had stolen my work and locked me out of my own community, yet I was supposed to just accept it?

No.

I couldn't apologize because I wasn't sorry. Not even a little.

To this day, though direct confrontation always tends to have an even worse outcome, I refuse to report people for bad behavior, always skeptical that "anonymous" actually means anonymous. I have endured some serious idiocy from inconsiderate or volatile neighbors over the years, gritting my teeth through thumping music, suspicious activity, and even the occasional property damage, solely because I was convinced that if I reported them, they would somehow find out it was me and retaliate.

But that day, reporting the site seemed like the only way to settle the score. It might've been hypocritical, but their content *did* violate the terms of service. And now, thanks to InsideTheWeb's brilliant handling of my report, there I was, denied once again any form of satisfaction or closure, sitting in my tiny apartment, contemplating my next move.

Patience has never been one of my virtues, but I let the new site and the sting of being exposed as the one who reported it stew for about a week before my next idea took shape. I needed time to regroup, to let my shame fade just enough so I could think clearly. More importantly, I wanted them to believe I had given up, that I had accepted my expulsion and moved on.

Once I was sure they had let their guard down, I put my plan into motion. Under a discreetly chosen pseudonym and as inconspicuously as possible, I submitted a new request for access to Paradise Isle. The timing was perfect. They had no reason to suspect anything, no lingering paranoia left from my report. This time, they let me in.

Bwaahahaaaaa. An evil plot is afoot.

I knew better than to charge in guns blazing, so I started slowly, subtly weaving my way into their ranks. I posted an introduction just like I had when I first joined LSB, only this time, the details were entirely fabricated. I gave a different age, different location, and different backstory. Nothing too dramatic, just enough to blend in, to sound authentic without drawing unnecessary attention.

The response was predictable. Just as they had welcomed me with open arms the first time around, they did so again, completely unaware. I played along, thanking them, engaging just enough to seem genuine, all while biding my time for the real fun to begin.

For my next move, I followed up with a fan fiction story I shamelessly lifted from a particularly naughty book of short stories Brenda had lent me. I changed just enough details to make it fit within the Leo-centric world of Paradise Isle, swapping out names, reworking a few descriptions, and inserting just the right amount of starry-eyed adoration. But the bones of it were stolen wholesale.

The storyline followed a couple playing tennis on an outdoor court at night when the lights go out with a loud pop, leading them to find other things to do behind the hedges. All I had to do was swap out the man's name for Leo's and voilà, I had an exciting but not-too-graphic tale of outdoor fun.

I reloaded the page obsessively, waiting for the first responses to roll in. Would they unwittingly swoon over the prose, the tension, and the way I captured the essence of their darling Leo participating in an illicit public activity?

They did.

They loved it. They ate it up. I could practically hear their keyboards clacking in anticipation as they begged for a follow-up.

The victory was hollow, overshadowed by regret. I hadn't thought this far ahead. I had been so focused on sneaking in, on proving I could still exist in the space they had tried so underhandedly to erase me from that I hadn't prepared for the emotional blow that followed.

I had unintentionally triggered that old, familiar feeling. It was the rush I used to get when I posted on Paradise Island, the high of seeing the positive feedback roll in, the validation that came with knowing my words had entertained someone. That sense of connection had been my lifeline for weeks before it was torn away. For just a brief second, I let myself sink into it, one last time.

In that moment, my heart broke all over again for what had been taken from me.

But then I looked around, scrolling through the usernames that had so graciously welcomed my plagiarized story, and I remembered. These weren't just faceless readers. These were the very people who had stolen Paradise Island, who had erased me from my own creation.

Regret erupted into blazing fury. I wasn't here for their approval. I was here to burn it all down.

The next day, I sat down to post again, determined to push the envelope even further. This time, I kicked the spice up a notch, crafting an over-the-top, brazenly inappropriate story that never would've made the cut on the old Paradise Island.

I spun a fitting tale about a woman shipwrecked on a tropical island, where she is captured by the natives and prepared as an offering to their king. Naturally, Leo had the lead role, emerging from a grass-roofed hut to inspect his prize, exuding the kind of untamed authority typical of an egotistical, domineering monarch.

From there, the scene plunged well beyond soft porn territory. It was so far beyond, in fact, that even my former coworker Brad would've needed a cold shower after reading it.

I should've known it would get pulled. I had lulled myself into a false sense of security after never seeing the moderators remove *anything*. Maybe they just didn't want to censor the board, or maybe they weren't paying as close attention as they used to. Either way, I had assumed I could test the boundaries without repercussions.

When it finally happened, I was stunned, but not because I thought it had been removed unfairly. I knew exactly what I had done. I was shocked they had finally drawn a line somewhere. I even tried to justify it, throwing out weak defenses about how it was just fantasy, and that the board had always been a place for creative expression. Predictably, I was scoffed at and dismissed without hesitation.

Because I had drawn attention to myself again and in a negative light, they took a closer look at my account, confirmed it was me under a new name, and promptly banned me from the Isle again. It was swift, decisive, and final. I had been caught red-handed, and they wasted no time making sure I was locked out for good.

I was chastised for my foolish attempt to stir up trouble, though no one seemed particularly surprised. My informant insisted they had known it was me all along, able to detect my personality from behind the mask of someone else's writing style. I never quite believed that and accepted it as an attempt to discourage me from trying something like that again.

But this time I didn't bother sneaking back on the Isle. I had done what I set out to do, mostly. I had something *akin* to closure, even if it hadn't ended in the satisfying destruction I had once envisioned. Instead, I tried to settle into life as a regular LSB contributor once more, swallowing my pride and pretending none of it had ever happened.

I became engrossed by interacting with every new LSB thread, trying to rekindle the sense of belonging I had lost. I thought I could get it back, but I grew restless. Something was missing. The pride that came with building, maintaining, and running my own space had been extinguished, and no amount of posting on someone else's message board could restore it.

I needed to create something new, something unique to the fandom with more to offer than a typical fan page. It also had to be entirely mine, with no need for moderators.

I had to ensure that whatever I created, it would be something no one could take from me this time.

Chapter 8: Uncharted Islands

"...THE OFFICIAL CYBER HOME OF LEONARDO DICAPRIO..." appeared in small white text against a stark black background, centered just below a glossy, bright blue navigation bar that stretched across the top of the page. Embedded within the blue bar were nine recessed, textured spheres, each serving as a clickable link. Bold yellow text in all capital letters labeled each sphere with standard offerings like News, Filmography, Awards, and Fan Club.

A large, triangular orange wedge with the word "Welcome" scrawled across it in cursive text featured prominently in the center, butted up against a behind-the-scenes photo of Leo from the set of *The Beach*. The entire design was a chaotic blend of bold colors, clashing textures, and sharp angles set in a fixed-width layout designed specifically to fill the tiny 800×600 monitor resolution that was standard at the time. For Y2K, it was cutting-edge.

I first stumbled across an earlier version of this very design about a year before, back when I was still stuck in the dark ages at the call center, before internet access was installed at my desk. It was shortly after seeing *Titanic* for the first time when gathering intelligence about my newfound obsession was all-consuming, but without daily internet access, it was slow going.

Determined to sign up for Leo's official fan club, I made a special trip to my mother's house to commandeer Jo Ann's computer for an hour. The fan club sat behind a $30 paywall, a one-time membership fee that seemed like a small fortune for a young woman in an entry-level job, but promised exclusive perks. Once inside, members gained access to a trove of rare photos and a simple JavaScript game that let you dress Leo like a paper doll, mixing and matching outfits in hopes of finding the right combination to advance to the next level. I never got past level one.

That $30 membership fee didn't just grant digital access. It also came with a physical welcome packet. Inside the colorful two-pocket folder was a collection of fan club goodies, including a printed membership certificate and an 8×10 glossy photo of Leo, his signature emblazoned across it in pre-printed ink. I felt like Ralphie excitedly tearing open his Little Orphan Annie decoder ring in *A Christmas Story*.

That was the closest to an actual autograph of his I ever owned, since the one I won on eBay, signed atop a still from *The Man in the Iron Mask*, was almost definitely fake. That was the thing about being a fan in the early internet era: you were always one click away from something thrilling, or an obvious scam. Every so often, something new would appear that was neither, a mystery waiting to be unraveled.

It was business as usual back on Leo's Sand Bar, as if the whole Paradise Island fiasco had never happened. The women who had defected to Paradise Isle mostly stayed in their own little corner of the internet, which meant I could navigate LSB freely without the awkwardness of running into them like an ex at the grocery store.

By the end of April 1999, *The Beach* was in post-production, so the steady trickle of set updates gave way to scattered sightings of Leo in Los Angeles. With no major projects on the horizon, the fans turned their attention elsewhere.

The latest obsession was the breaking gossip that Leo had broken up with his long-time girlfriend, Kristen Zang. LSB members studied every badly lit paparazzi photo in which some unsuspecting young woman happened to appear in the same frame as Leo. They assessed each shot for signs of a possible love connection, or rather, the blessed absence of one, as if it were a full-time occupation.

A few women on LSB scolded the rest of us for celebrating his newly-single status, self-righteously insisting they'd rather see him settled down and happy. Trolls chimed in to remind us that no fan from the bowels of flyover country would ever end up with him, as if that thought had never crossed our minds. None of us truly believed we'd catch his eye in real life or that we'd hit it off even if we did, but knowing he was unattached nudged the daydream just far enough into the faint realm of possibility to keep the fantasy alive. And that fantasy, that distraction, was all any of us really wanted.

Then, one day that spring, a notice appeared on Leo's official website, teasing a new chat room feature coming in early summer to the paid-access fan club pages. The announcement promised scheduled chats with special guests, offering fan club members an unprecedented opportunity to interact with people from Leo's inner circle. The first guest in the lineup was promised to be Leo's mother.

The excitement on LSB was instantly electric. We dubbed it the "O Chat" on the "O Site," shortening the word "official" without considering how it sounded. Some fans were blissfully unaware of the obvious double entendre, but it was the first thing I thought of every time someone said it. Considering how many of us had already posted some very impure thoughts about Leo, though, it felt hilariously appropriate.

It wasn't long before I noticed a common theme in the discussions on LSB. Several fans admitted they had never been in a chat room before and were anxious about how it all worked. Some worried about keeping up with the conversation, while others weren't even sure how to log in. It was a problem just waiting for someone to solve…

EUREKA! I could build a chat room!

I had been searching for a reason to take another shot at a fan site, but I needed something unique that would make it feel worthwhile. This was it: a practice chat room where fans could get comfortable with the new format before the real thing. There would be no paywall and no scheduled guests, just a relaxed, pressure-free space to figure out the basics.

The range of web-building tools available for WebTV users was surprisingly impressive. Most of it was the usual fare, but then, buried among the familiar options of GIF makers and graphics collections, I was shocked to find exactly what I needed.

A company referring to itself as an "online community provider" called Talk City had created a WebTV-friendly chat room service. It could provide a free, fully functional chat room I could integrate directly into my own site. My little practice chat room idea had just gone from "I'm not sure that's possible for someone stuck with WebTV" to "this is happening before I log off today!"

Setting up a chat room was shockingly easy. Webmasters could sign up, stake out a dedicated space for their site, and have it up and running in minutes. Once reserved, it functioned like a private group chat in a client like Microsoft Teams, though without any message history.

On the left side of the screen, a list of active users updated in real time, while the larger chat window on the right displayed messages as they were posted. Beneath that, a smaller text-entry box and a bright SEND button made the setup feel simple and intuitive.

For extra privacy, you could select a user from the list on the left and switch the chat mode to private, making your messages visible only to that person. But this feature came with a dangerous flaw. A single accidental extra click, easier to do than you'd think, could leave you believing you were whispering in secrecy when, in reality, your messages were still broadcasting to the entire room. It was a ticking time bomb for embarrassing slip-ups, and plenty of people learned that lesson the hard way.

Once you signed up for the service, the final step was copying a short snippet of code and pasting it onto your GeoCities homepage. Instantly, a simple login box appeared on your page, allowing visitors to enter their name and click a button to jump straight into the room. New visitors didn't even have to sign up for a permanent account before they could enter.

In the years since this experience, I've tried recreating the magic by setting up other pop culture-themed chat rooms, but once social media arrived, nothing could compete with it. Fandoms thrive on platforms where conversations leave a public record, where fans can have at least a little hope that the object of their enthusiasm might later see their posts and interact with them.

In a traditional chat room, that kind of interaction only happened if the celebrity showed up in real time. In 1999, that was almost unheard of, especially in fan-run spaces. There was no such thing as a celebrity liking your post, retweeting your thoughts, or commenting directly at you.

Fame made people far more inaccessible then. None of us realized we were living in the twilight of the untouchable, ethereal celebrity. But even now, when many of his contemporaries regularly engage with fans across various platforms, Leo remains distant, choosing instead to release only polished, professionally worded statements on his official accounts, undoubtedly posted by a social media manager under the watchful eye of a publicist.

This chat room wasn't meant to attract anyone famous, least of all Leo, whose social calendar alone was surely so jam-packed he'd never have time for such foolishness. Even if someone did show up claiming to be famous, it would be nearly impossible to verify. I just wanted something of my own to nurture, something I could cultivate and watch grow, like Paradise Island had started to do. Even a minor success was better than another failure.

Whatever happened, I had learned my lesson. This time, I would be the only moderator and webmaster, and I wasn't giving anyone else the access to lock me out of it.

I created "The Cabana," a site intended as sort of an annex of LSB, a simplistic meeting place with none of the bells or whistles I tried to implement on DiCaprio Street. The chat's login box appeared right in the center of the otherwise bare homepage. There were no extra features to draw attention away from the primary purpose of the site, no photo gallery or message board. Nothing but the chat itself.

As I had done after building Paradise Island, I obtained Richard's permission before I posted the link on the LSB message board, promoting it as a place for fans to get comfortable with chatting before the O Chats began and as an after-party lounge to go to at the end of each scheduled chat. Then I sat back, watching the empty room, waiting to see who would be the first to show up.

By the time I set up The Cabana, I had been unemployed for a couple of months, living in that uneasy limbo where each passing week without a paycheck made survival feel like a tightrope act. Somehow, my landlord never seemed to notice that I hadn't paid the back rent, or if she did, she chose to ignore it, ensuring I could at least hold onto my independence.

She handed the property management over to her nephew a few months after I moved in, but she conveniently neglected to tell him about our prior arrangement. I finally landed a new job about a month after setting up the chat, so I was already making regular payments by the time he took over the books. The three months of missed rent payments slipped through the cracks and were never mentioned again, providing the first stability I had felt in months.

But for now, I had an entire month with nothing to do but sit in my new chat room waiting for visitors to appear. I knew the key to a real-time chat's success was consistency. Someone had to be there, ready to engage with new people who wandered in. So I kept the chat room open on my television all afternoon and evening while I went about life in the rest of the apartment, doing housework or some other such thing.

I would check the screen from time to time to make sure I hadn't missed a notification, only to find I was still alone in the room. The moment I heard the familiar bling alerting me to a new chatter, I sprinted across the apartment to the sofa. There, my wireless keyboard rested on a wooden TV tray which functioned as my makeshift WebTV command center.

I greeted every visitor with as much energy as I could muster. I asked leading questions about how they found the chat, what they thought of Leo, and really anything to keep the conversation flowing. Some were shy, others were enthusiastic to discuss *anything* about the man of the hour, but no matter who popped in, I wanted them to feel welcome and entertained enough to stay.

I was beginning to recognize that my social awkwardness may have played a bigger role in the Paradise Island incident than I realized, because now it was making it tough to hold a visitor's attention when I was the only one in the chat room. Still, I gave it everything I had, filling silences with questions and hoping for responses longer than one-word answers.

Things got easier in the evenings, just after dinner, when traffic picked up. Once two people were chatting, it was much easier to keep a third engaged, so I often lured people into staying longer by promising more chatters would be along shortly to make it more of a party. In a chat room, the more, the merrier, or at least, that's how it was supposed to work.

Although it wasn't an instant hit on day one, little by little, several names began appearing more often, until they became familiar visitors. It wasn't the thriving message board community I had tried to build before, but it offered an ease that Paradise Island's forum never could. The constant pressure to produce new fan fiction and drive engagement had made Paradise Island feel more like a job than a hobby.

In relatively short order, a core group of regulars had formed, keeping The Cabana active for hours every evening, with or without my help. Within a week or two, the room had become nearly self-sustaining, and I was back in the saddle. Giddy up!

Chapter 9: Jumping the Falls

The spring of 1999 saw life on LSB rolling along much as it always had, full of speculation, gossip, and the usual debates over the latest photographs. Over on Paradise Isle, my former friends continued churning out their lusty daydream compositions behind the locked door of their secured message board. Meanwhile, something entirely different was taking shape in The Cabana chat room.

One by one, the cast of characters who would come to define the next year of my life began appearing, each adding their own splash of personality and flavor to the cocktail that would become The Cabana, our own little beachside retreat. Some were occasional visitors, others would eventually become treasured friends, but together, they would make the chat room feel like a world of its own.

The first regular to make herself at home in the chat was Kim, a 55-year-old redheaded firecracker from South Carolina where she lived with her husband and pre-teen son. We found our common ground almost immediately. Her husband had inherited his parents' lake house, just over an hour's drive from Knoxville, and her family used it as a vacation spot a few times a year. That small connection made our conversations feel less like trivial online chatter and more like something rooted in real life.

Kim's energy was feisty, bursting with sass and panache. She had a sarcastic tongue but a warm heart, ready at any moment with a playful jab or an exaggerated sigh over the latest Leo gossip. If the chat room were a movie, the only actor who could do Kim justice would be Allison Janney.

When we finally met for lunch in Knoxville during her next trip to Tennessee, she arrived with the same bold presence she carried in the chat room and introduced me to her drink of choice, Cold Duck, a burgundy sparkling wine often marketed as a holiday indulgence. Kim, however, saw no reason to limit it to special occasions. Even after more than a quarter century, I still occasionally pick up a bottle and drink a toast to her, a private tribute to the friendship we built. After all, she was almost as much a fixture in the chat room as I was.

Next came Kelly, a soft-spoken, kind-hearted woman in her 30s from Australia, who tiptoed into the chat room with a blend of curiosity and hesitation. The time difference meant she spent her afternoons with us while we were deep into our evenings.

Kelly wasn't the most outspoken, often preferring to observe, but there was a subdued sweetness in the way she engaged, like someone testing the water before fully diving in. As the days passed and she warmed up, her messages grew longer. Her responses were less hesitant but always with a slight timidity. She was as meek as a church mouse, excitable in the cutest little squeaking way.

Not long after, Gwen joined the fray, a middle-aged woman from somewhere in the sweeping sprawl of Midwestern America. In hindsight, she was so unremarkable that I struggle to recall much about her at all. She blended in seamlessly, participating like any other fan, typically never commanding attention. She chatted about Leo, shared her thoughts on the latest gossip, and reacted to other people's stories without adding many of her own. If she had strong opinions, she kept them to herself. Back then, she seemed like a background character to fill the spaces. But looking back, maybe that was the point.

Adding to the fun were Matthew and Tiffany, a young married couple in their early 20s from Alberta, Canada, who brought an easygoing, playful spirit to the chat. They described their home office as two desks arranged facing away from each other, the chairs positioned back-to-back between them, the wheels nearly intermingling each time one of them pushed themselves away from their desk to stand up. It was an arrangement that let them type away while stealing glances at each other's screens.

Their dynamic made them feel like a unit, two halves of the same witty whole. Whether they were teasing each other or jumping into the latest Leo debate, they were always up for a laugh, and their warmth was infectious.

Rounding out our little crew of regulars was Bobby, a single parent from Philadelphia with a complicated introduction to the group. He had already stirred up some drama over on LSB, where he initially posed as a woman, worried he'd be judged for participating in fan discussions about Leo. With barely any other guys around (besides Matthew, of course), he assumed he'd be mocked or his sexuality would be questioned for participating in a fandom dedicated to a young man.

By the time he found his way to the chat room, he was already "out" as himself. He crept in cautiously, half-expecting side-eye and cold shoulders, worried that his past deception would follow him. Instead, he was met with little more than teasing and the occasional joke, treated more like a wayward friend than a pariah. Bobby embraced his place in the group, carving out his own niche as one of the only men in our little online world.

His lack of confidence and limited education sometimes made it difficult to tell if Bobby was even an adult. His messages could be immature, his spelling shaky, and his reactions impulsive to the point that, for a while, I genuinely wondered if he might be a preteen pretending to be older. It wasn't until someone from LSB met him in person and confirmed that, yes, he was a grown man, I finally let go of that suspicion.

Even so, his emotional streak could tank the room's mood in an instant. When he felt the need for attention he would try to steer the conversation toward himself, often with a dramatic story about some offline personal crisis that seemed just a little too convenient. As much as I wanted to believe he had turned over a new leaf, his earlier deception made it difficult to trust his stories.

If Bobby was the only source of drama at The Cabana, I could live with that. After what happened with Paradise Island, a little emotional turbulence was nothing.

After about 6 p.m. on any given weekday evening, there was almost always at least a few of us in the chat, catching up on the day, swapping stories, venting about life, or weighing in on someone's latest personal dilemma. Despite being a Leo fan chat, actual discussions about Leo were rare.

Instead, we talked about everything else from family drama, work gripes, the latest episode of *Friends* or *The X-Files*, to whatever movie someone had just rented from Blockbuster. The only time Leo's name really came up was when a new chatter wandered in, eager to gush about the latest gossip. We humored them, of course, but for us, the real appeal of the chat wasn't Leo. It was each other.

Most nights, it was just us regulars, unless someone reposted the link on LSB, drawing in a stray newcomer or two. That suited us fine. The relaxed, comfortable atmosphere made it easier to have personal conversations without feeling like we were performing for an audience. Weekends, though, were a different story. The room filled up with familiar faces from LSB, many of whom lingered for an hour or so before withdrawing back into the vast, ever-churning fandom. The chat never reached the size or activity of Paradise Island at its prime, but that was exactly why it worked. It wasn't a fan hub. It was better… it was a home.

Before we knew it, the day of the first O Chat had arrived. I don't remember exactly how I found out that the new official chat room wasn't compatible with WebTV, but I knew I needed a backup plan. Fortunately, Brenda had a desktop computer, and she had agreed to let me borrow it while she was out for the evening.

She greeted me at the door on her way out, offering a casual wave before pulling the door shut behind her, leaving me alone in the stillness of her empty apartment. I paused a moment, then peeked through the blinds and watched as she strolled across the parking lot toward her car.

The moment her taillights disappeared down the street, I clumsily bounded over to her desk in the corner of her dining room, full of anxious anticipation. I took a deep breath as I eased into the chair behind the computer desk, then clicked the button to connect to her America Online dial-up service and waited for the familiar whine of the modem.

"Beep-beep-beep-beeeeeep," pulsed the dial tone. With dial-up internet service you could hear the phone's dial tone before the computer's modem attempted to dial out. Typically the tone was composed of two clashing frequencies that blended together to form a single unbroken tone to indicate to the user (or in this case, the computer) that the line was available and working before dialing the number.

My apologies to readers born before 2000, who may have just had the horrifying realization that we now have to explain what a dial tone was.

I had forgotten that Brenda had the TouchStar feature on her landline, a premium service that included a voicemail box. When a new message was waiting, the dial tone stuttered for the first few seconds after the handset was picked up. Unbeknownst to me, this also caused her computer's modem to think the line was dead. It refused to connect, and I didn't have her access code to clear the new message notification. Brenda was long gone and she didn't have a cell phone. None of my friends did back then.

Pandemonium ensued.

I paced around her apartment with clenched fists, resisting the urge to wring my hands like some frantic villain in an old movie. If anyone had seen the look on my face, they'd probably have thought I'd just accidentally committed a murder and was panicking over where to hide the body.

I tried to connect again… no go. It wouldn't even try.

"All this work to get ready and *I'M GOING TO MISS IT!!*"

I don't recall if I was screaming in my head or out loud… or both. My whole body was tense with agitation, drenched with nervous sweat, and the only thing I could hear was my own heartbeat in my ears. This was so preventable, so stupid, and yet I had walked right into it. And the worst part? There wasn't even anyone to be mad at. No one had sabotaged me, it was just dumb luck. Well, except the universe. That, I could absolutely blame for cursing me with this unbelievable calamity.

And then, just as I was on the brink of a full mental breakdown, it hit me. Anyone who grew up with a landline knew the struggle of multiple extensions, when your mom would pick up the phone in another room and start dialing before realizing you were on the line. I could use the phone's handset to connect to the line, let the stuttered tone play out, and then, once the steady dial tone returned, click to connect the dial-up.

It didn't work. I missed the chat.

Defeated and furious with myself for not making sure the dial-up connected before Brenda left, I skulked back to my apartment and logged into LSB. For the next hour, I sat refreshing the deserted message board, as if waiting for my class to return from a field trip I'd forgotten my permission slip for.

When the O Chat was over, participants were still buzzing with adrenaline and eager to keep chatting. The official room had been closed at the end of the event, kicking everyone out before they'd had their fill. They streamed into The Cabana to burn off the excess energy and report on what had gone on, like kids going out for ice cream after a grade-school recital.

There had been a few technical problems and a guest limit the chatmaster had been unaware of that kept dozens of people stuck out in the virtual cold, but it had been an overall success. One of the women captured the chat text before logging off and posted the transcript on LSB, which, I supposed, was better than nothing for those of us who missed out.

The chat was hosted by a user with the handle "Birken," from Birken Interactive Studios, Leo's original production company that had just been formed earlier that year. It had been named after his mother, Irmelin Indenbirken, which was fitting for this particular occasion. At the beginning of the chat session, Birken announced that the entire company, a list of 10 employees *including* Irmelin, were in attendance for this inaugural chat.

The accidental guest limit of 25 had kept the first chat surprisingly low-key, though a couple of the ladies nervously spammed the room with random chatter, unsure of what to say. After Irmelin answered a few questions and handed the Birken account back to the unnamed staffer running the chat that night, the account fell silent. For a moment, the room took on the tone of a group of friends awkwardly trying to make conversation with a shy stranger they were stuck in an elevator with.

That is, until it was announced that Leo had arrived at the Birken offices and was taking over the Birken handle. He had made a special trip to the office especially to launch his brand-new chat room in person.

And I. Missed. It.

His visit was brief, only a few lines of text before declaring he had to take a call, but he had been there, and all my friends had been with him. But not me.

The next O Chat was scheduled just a few days later. It was announced as an off-schedule session with no special guests, meant only to test changes and correct settings. I took the opportunity to stay at my apartment and attempt to join using WebTV, but, as expected, it didn't work.

When the transcript was posted to LSB afterward, I found that my desperation had been witnessed by everyone in the room. The chat room had announced my attempted entrances multiple times before I blindly declared that I couldn't see any messages, asked that someone post the transcript to LSB when it ended, and finally retreated back to The Cabana while the O Chat rolled on without me, once again.

That was the last straw. I had put up with WebTV's limitations for long enough, and not being able to participate in the O Chats was simply intolerable. As the owner of one of the more active websites in the fandom, I saw myself as a kind of community leader, with an obligation to stay informed of all the latest goings-on. I didn't care that I was still unemployed, I needed a *real* computer. Impulsively, I went straight to Gateway Computers' website, filled out an application for a credit line, and hit submit.

Somehow, despite my complete lack of income, they approved me. I prefer to think of it as tenacious sales tactics rather than predatory lending, choosing to ignore the fact that it would inevitably result in snowballing late fees. It was a decision that would haunt me and my credit score for years. The only thing that mattered in that moment was securing my access to the O Chats. Within minutes, I had placed an order for the first home computer that was truly, entirely mine.

A week later, two big boxes stamped with Gateway's distinctive black-and-white cow print logo landed on my front doorstep. I giddily dragged them inside, barely able to believe I finally had a real computer of my very own. Until then, my second bedroom had been mostly used as a storage space, but now, it had a purpose. I set it up as an office, pushing a small desk against the wall and making the back of the apartment my new command center.

There had been something oddly comforting about using WebTV from the sofa, the way I still felt connected to the real world by listening to the goings-on in the parking lot through the windows behind my head as I chatted. But now, I had a dedicated workspace and a capable machine. Now, I meant business. My friends would be lucky if they ever saw me again.

The new computer arrived just in time for me to join the third O Chat, giving me a courtside view of the effects the updated configurations had. With a much higher guest limit, messages rocketed up and off the screen at a pace that seemed to catch even the chatmaster off guard.

"I'm the chatmaster, but Vlad and Lynn are here," an unnamed member of the Birken staff announced as the chat began. The anonymous staffer tried to steer the conversation but quickly fell behind. They silently watched the bedlam for long stretches, only occasionally replying to whatever comment happened to pause on the screen long enough to be read.

The O Chats that followed moved at a similar pace, with the role of chatmaster rotating between characters named Felix, Jubei, HLime, Jonah, and Vlad, among others, who often filled the silence with silly, off-topic banter. Over the next few months, Irmelin continued to pop in occasionally, joined eventually by Jerry Swindall, an actor who played one of the backpackers Leo's character Richard had given a map to in *The Beach*.

Of the four months' worth of O Chats for which any record still exists, Leo only appeared as himself, at most, three times. During his last "official" appearance in the room, he admitted that he often lurked without participating, or stood over the chatmaster's shoulder watching the madness from afar. The chatmaster also revealed during the first O Chat that the room was created because Leo "loves chat rooms." The allure of anonymity must have been powerful, but never knowing when or if he might be watching was nerve-wracking.

Once all of the LSB regulars had worked out their issues with the O Chat, life at The Cabana settled into a comfortable, laid-back groove. Regulars drifted in and out, conversations weaved from the day's minutiae to whatever outlandish topic caught our fancy and someone was always there, ready to welcome you in.

At long last, I'd found my own "Monica's apartment," a place where I genuinely belonged.

We collectively sank into the coziness of familiarity and companionship, blissfully unaware that we were on the verge of something incredible that none of us would ever forget.

Chapter 10: Tides Turning Tables

By the time the temp agency placed me in a job they said would be "easy data entry" after three months of unemployment, the summer of 1999 was already underway. The job landed me in a regional office of an international media company, a branch of a much larger corporation that also happened to own assets in Hollywood. It wasn't exactly compelling work, but it came with one unexpected perk. The Global Address List on our computers was stacked with some surprisingly well-known names.

Had I been reckless enough to risk my brand-new job, I could have easily reached out to someone who, without question, had a direct line to Leo.

The office was on the east side of town, opposite the direction most people took at rush hour in Knoxville. For once, my daily commute was a breeze, but there was a catch. This was the "bad" side of town, the kind of seedy area with more bail bonds offices, pawn shops, and payday lenders than fast food joints.

The building itself was an aging two-story structure directly off the main highway, with barely enough parking for the 40 employees inside. Most of the main floor was a mix of conference rooms and private offices, except for a small area of cubicles where the data entry temps were assigned. The second floor was a small call center, split between customer service and sales functions.

The building's floorplan seemed to shape the business management structure, with the call center upstairs operating almost like a separate tenant. Downstairs was simply known as "the office," home to ten employees, not counting the district manager. Technically, she was the office manager's boss and oversaw everyone, but she never really felt like part of our team. When she wasn't out in the field, she spent her time secluded in a large corner office, shut-in with floor-to-ceiling windows framing a view of the parking lot from the building behind ours.

There were only four data entry cubicles, two of which had been taken over for storage. Mine was wedged next to the main conference room door, with my back to the steady stream of field managers and salespeople coming in for meetings. I hated the lack of privacy, but it gave me the perfect stage to show off my best office skill.

I had learned to type on that old Tandy 1000 years earlier, using a *Space Invaders*-style typing game that provided one of the few skills I had that impressed people, learning to type fast enough to avoid being blown up by letters falling down from above. The field managers often gathered behind me, watching as I keyed in the data off the work orders and sales forms their field staff sent in, marveling at the speed at which my fingers moved. I may not have had much administrative experience, but I was top of my class at shooting letters.

My new role involved keying in customer payment and sales records, survey responses, tracking logs, and whatever other bits of data showed up in the never-ending stack of paperwork that materialized in my inbox as if by magic. The work was mind-numbingly tedious, but at least I wasn't arguing with irate customers about appliance parts anymore. That alone made it feel like an upgrade, even though my desk had no permanent internet connection.

Transmitting the data I had so efficiently entered to headquarters required ensuring the phone line was free. The data entry terminals were configured to dial-up using the same line the district manager used for voice calls when she was in the office, so I had to coordinate the uploads with her field time. The whole thing felt like being back at home, waiting for Mom to get off the phone so I could connect to AOL.

Thanks to The Cabana chat room, I had already kicked my addiction to the Leo's Sand Bar message board, but the new job kept me far too busy to notice anyway. Browsing the board at work had once been a daily craving, but I barely even missed it now. I didn't even have time to think about what could be happening in the chat room. It helped that the chat regulars were rarely online during the day, so there wasn't much FOMO because there was nothing happening to fear missing out on.

The appliance call center had always left me drained to my core. There's something about being surrounded by constant discontent that wears down not just your mind, but your whole body. The endless barrage of complaints, demands, and frustration had taken its toll, and I hadn't even realized just how much until I was finally free of it. I had needed those three months off to heal from the burnout.

Going back to a nine-to-five routine afterward wasn't easy, but having some stability again lifted a huge weight off my shoulders. By the end of my first week at the media office, I felt almost rejuvenated. It was a feeling I hadn't associated with work in a long time. When I got home Friday evening, I was ready to kick back, settle into my usual comfy chair in the corner of the chat room, and spend the entire weekend unwinding with my new friends.

The gang was already assembled and deep in conversation by the time I logged in after dinner. Kim was mid-story, probably halfway through her first bottle of Cold Duck, holding court with Matthew, Tiff, and Gwen as she cryptically hinted at having insider knowledge about the true identities of the Birken chatmasters, intel the rest of us supposedly couldn't obtain.

Kim loved playing the Gatekeeper, always implying she had access to a covert channel the rest of us were locked out of. To an outsider, it might have seemed like a manipulation tactic, a way to draw attention through exclusivity. But Kim was audacious in her own right and didn't need gimmicks to command a room. At The Cabana, she was simply playing her part, adding to the intrigue spun by the elusive chatmasters of the O Chat.

By the time Kim's story finally wrapped up, Kelly had joined in, bubbling with excitement over a new behind-the-scenes photo of a shirtless Leo from the set of *The Beach* that had just surfaced on LSB. Naturally, we had to see it for ourselves. After we'd each gotten our eyes full, we drifted back into the chat, where the conversation spiraled into an impromptu roleplay session inspired by the bare-skinned snapshot.

We all took turns pretending to be a team of masseuses giving Leo a massage, except for Matthew, who wanted no part of it. Each of us claimed a body part, describing in absurd detail how it felt beneath our hands. It was surprisingly entertaining and had all the hallmarks of Paradise Island-style escapism, though compared to that, this was downright wholesome.

I was already cringing from the familiarity of this sort of topic when a new name blinked into the user list on the left-hand side of the chat window.

Blungo has entered the chat.

Hmm. Someone we'd never seen before… a "24-year-old guy from California," he introduced himself.

Gwen. Lost. Her. Mind.

"Are you Leo? Are you sure you're not Leo? You sound like you could be Leo," she rapid-fired, barely letting him breathe as he tried to settle in.

He handled it well, unflappable and calm, brushing it off. "Nope, definitely not Leo. Just Blungo." But Gwen wasn't letting it go.

I toggled on the private chat feature and shot her a message. "*Knock it off. If it is him, he won't like being pestered like that. Just pretend he's just another chatter, same as anybody else.*"

Gwen reluctantly backed off, though I could practically feel the room crackling with her excitement. Blungo's vibe, on the other hand, seemed to relax a little. We eased back into the conversation as Blungo observed our interactions.

"Blungo," as he later explained, was an intentionally flubbed version of "Bungo" from the British kids' show *The Wombles*. He never elaborated on why he picked it, if *The Wombles* actually had some sentimental significance to him, or why he had chosen to alter the name.

"You know Leo's had professional massages." Blungo interjected, sounding a little embarrassed by the topic of conversation. It did seem ridiculous that he'd be getting one from a pack of silly fans.

"THIGHS," I blurted out, reserving my favorite of Leo's body parts for this virtual massage.

"Oh. You're *that* one," Blungo replied, teasing me in a way that practically radiated a smirk.

I didn't want to overreact. I didn't want to fall for a hoax, what could've been my first brush with something we now know as catfishing, but this person just felt *different.*

It was the odd way he dropped details that lined up a little too perfectly with Leo, yet kept denying it. He didn't act like a fan. He offered no gossiping, no over-the-top devotion, not even a passing comment about what he liked about Leo's movies, nor did he act like a troll just visiting to mess with Leo's admirers.

And, he'd been watching us.

He knew me by my obsession with Leo's thighs, something I'd only mentioned semi-publicly in the O Chat a week earlier. Whoever had been wearing the Birken hat that day went silent for several minutes, allowing the conversation between fans to carry on unabated. The production company staff was undoubtedly sitting back and watching in amusement as we once again spiraled into a discussion that included mentions of Leo's body parts.

"THIGHS" had started as a bit I reserved for the relative privacy of The Cabana, but that day, I'd been bold enough to unleash it behind the O Chat paywall. Most of the regulars there were also familiar faces from LSB, so it's hard to say, all these years later, whether I was just goofing off among friends or putting on a show for whoever at Birken might have been watching, maybe even Leo himself.

But Blungo never once hinted at why he was even lurking on a Leonardo DiCaprio fan site, let alone whether or not he had a paid fan club membership with access to the O Chat.

Another thing gnawed at me. There were hardly any men on these forums, yet I already had two male regulars… and now here was another? I couldn't help it. I had to entertain the possibility.

Could it be? Was Blungo, in fact, *Leo*?

Blungo had shamelessly flirted with me during the standard A/S/L exchange (Age/Sex/Location, the original icebreaker of the early World Wide Web), teasing that he "liked older girls" once he realized I was just a few months older than him. That might seem to disprove the theory that Leo and Blungo were the same person given Leo's now meme-worthy reputation for dating younger women. Yet at the time, his most recent girlfriend, whom he dated for four years before breaking up not long after filming *The Beach*, was five months older than him.

The only thing we knew for sure was that, real or not, we had to act like we didn't notice anything different about him. If he was going to stick around, he needed to feel like just another chatter. He hung out for about an hour, and when he finally logged out, the room fell into a heavy silence as we collected ourselves.

We *all* felt it.

He had been tactical… careful, even cagey He'd dropped just enough breadcrumbs for plausible deniability, making sure we couldn't prove it, couldn't even talk about it without sounding completely unhinged, with just enough uncertainty to make us doubt our own instincts.

I don't remember who broke the silence first, but we all agreed. If it wasn't Leo, it was a very unusual way to behave, even for a trickster attempting to perpetrate a hoax.

I sprang into action, updating the homepage to add "Room Rules" right above the login box. Rule number one: No pestering new users with 20 different variations of "Are you Leo?"

We had been lucky he didn't leave as soon as Gwen laid into him, and we had to ensure that never happened again. Besides, it was just good manners.

The only question now was, would "Blungo" return?

Chapter 11: Hard Coded Karma

My family didn't get cable television until the summer I turned 15 years old in 1989. Until then, we relied on an old rooftop antenna and a prayer, hoping the signal would hold steady long enough to catch something watchable. The channels we did get were often a mess, with static snow and an occasional rolling screen that required someone to fiddle with the vertical hold knob

When we finally got cable, it felt like stepping into another world. That entire first summer, I barely left my parents' bedroom, glued to the tiny 13-inch color TV my dad had bought to replace the old black-and-white set he had repurposed as the TRS-80 monitor years before.

MTV and Nickelodeon were my two favorite channels. I was entranced by the video for Fine Young Cannibals' song *She Drives Me Crazy* and loved *Grimm's Fairy Tale Classics*, especially the "Briar Rose" episode, which to this day remains the only anime I've ever enjoyed. I had no idea that was even a genre at the time.

Another favorite was a quirky yet hilarious eight-minute animated short that Nickelodeon kept on rotation for when the scheduled programming ran long. It was about a man named Mr. Johnson, who rescues a seemingly sweet little yellow cat, only to discover it's a holy terror. Hell-bent on exorcising the beast from his home by any means necessary, Mr. Johnson tries everything to get rid of it, from dropping it off in the middle of nowhere to more *extreme* measures. Yet no matter how many times he thought he had finally escaped its grasp, he'd return home to find it already waiting for him, its beady little eyes brimming with mischief.

The name of the short? *The Cat Came Back.*

Yes, yes, he did.

The very next evening, as a matter of fact. Shortly after I logged in, there he was.

Blungo has entered the chat.

He noticed the newly posted room rules right above the login box and promptly sent me a private message to thank me, since I had introduced myself as the site owner the night before. I took the opportunity to apologize for Gwen's little foible when he first arrived. He calmly dismissed it as if he had expected it.

That night, the conversation took a more personal turn. One by one, everyone in the chat began sharing stories about where they grew up. We described our hometowns, childhood memories, and the little details that made each place unique.

Blungo seemed genuinely interested, asking follow-up questions and engaging with all of us like he wanted to know more. But while he was happy to listen, he didn't offer much about himself in return. It was a subtle thing, but nothing he did went unnoticed. He was curious about our lives but kept his own cards close to his chest, a fact we all found deliciously suspicious.

When it was my turn, I described that tranquil little place built into the side of a ridge where I was raised, nestled next door to a small tobacco farm, with a cow pasture stretching out over the hillside across the road from the mailbox at the end of our long gravel driveway.

There was a brief pause.

"There are cows in Tennessee?!" Blungo said in surprise.

I smirked at my screen. You don't have to tell *me* who's a city boy.

I've spent the last 25 years wishing I had kept a diary, a meticulous record of when Blungo appeared, what he said, and how each interaction unfolded… because this was far from his last visit. It would have been so easy to copy the chat text after he left the room, to preserve it for posterity, to have something concrete to look back on instead of relying on the faulty, frustrating nature of memory. Yet, I didn't, and not because the thought never crossed my mind. It did, more than once. I *intentionally* chose not to.

It felt like a breach of trust, a violation of an unspoken rule. He never asked us not to save anything. He never hinted at wanting our conversations to be private. And yet, something about hitting "Save" felt wrong. If I didn't feel compelled to save anyone else's conversations, then I shouldn't save his, either.

I know it was a silly concern. Nothing we talked about was earth-shattering. If anything, most of it would have been boring to any die-hard fan hoping for juicy revelations. And even if I had saved every word, he never would have known.

But in that moment, none of that mattered.

What mattered was meeting the moment with integrity. What mattered was ensuring that, no matter what happened next, I wouldn't look back in the years to come and regret the way I handled it.

Because if I knew anything, I knew I would always remember these chats.

I've scoured every memory I have of those chats trying to pin down the exact time frame of Blungo's visits, but without that documentation, the details are frustratingly elusive. My heart remembers it as a brief, electric burst in time that may have lasted just two or three whirlwind weeks, but logic tells me it must have stretched out much longer.

Perhaps his appearances blended so naturally into our routine that my mind stitched them together into a tidy linear sequence of key moments, a *CliffsNotes* version of our association. Yet the fragments of our conversations that still exist in my memory reference different times of year or specific events pointing to a timeline that was more likely to have stretched over at least a few months.

Either way, for a little while, he was just another regular at The Cabana. Or at least, we tried really hard to think of him that way. He wasn't even a daily visitor and his visits were usually brief, typically no more than an hour at a time, but he was still one of us.

Of all Blungo's visits and the countless random conversations we had, only two moments ever made me pause, *really pause*, in my cautious-but-optimistic belief that he was exactly who he kept insisting he wasn't. The first questionable moment came almost immediately, during this second visit.

As conversations often do, ours meandered down winding side roads, veering from one topic to another, sometimes without any real connection between them. Inside jokes, tangents, and long-winded stories were the norm.

During a lull in conversation, Tiffany made an announcement. "BRB, grabbing a fresh bottle of Snapple."

It was a throwaway line, the kind of thing no one would normally dwell on, let alone remember years later, but Blungo's response landed like a needle ripping across a vinyl record.

"You've been reading about me," Blungo said, matter-of-factly.

The chat stopped cold.

Everyone must've clocked the misstep at the exact same time, a speechless, collective realization rippling through the room. We all froze, waiting for someone, anyone, to say something and break the deafening silence.

Before anyone could react, Blungo steered the conversation right back to the topic of our childhood homes, as if nothing unusual had just slipped out.

Um… *what?*

The comment just didn't sit right. It was the way he said it. "You've been reading about me." The phrasing was unnerving, almost accusatory. Why had he assumed Tiffany's mention of Snapple had anything to do with him? I didn't fully catch the meaning until later, after Blungo had logged off for the night.

Curious, I did a little digging. I pulled out one of those "Leo's Favorite Things" lists, the kind that filled every fan magazine and cheap paperback biography covered with his *Titanic*-era face. And there it was.

Leo's favorite drink: Snapple.

Matthew later confirmed that Tiffany had, in fact, simply meant that she was grabbing a fresh drink. There was no hidden meaning and no wink-wink nod to Leo trivia, just a regular person getting a Snapple

What haunted me about it was how Blungo, who had been so restrained during his first visit, had stumbled so easily this time. The gaffe felt almost too on-the-nose. It was exactly the kind of thing a sloppy imposter might say, yet also something a clever one might throw out just to test the waters. Could it be the real Leo intentionally allowing his mask to slip just enough to tease us, too? Surely not. He *is* said to have a wicked sense of humor, though. After all, if Blungo was Leo, he would have already assumed we suspected him, no matter how many times he denied it.

What made him stand out was what he *didn't* say. Everything we believed about who he was came from our own reading between the lines. He wasn't disruptive or fishing for attention. He never asked for anything. If he *was* an imposter, no one could figure out what he stood to gain.

Though we tried to treat Blungo like just one of the guys, the knowledge of who he probably was clung to the edges of every conversation, unspoken but unmistakably there. We kept telling ourselves we were too cool to fangirl, but this was a chat room for Leonardo DiCaprio fans in the middle of *Leomania*, after all.

We were trying not to make fools of ourselves in our very own digital version of the birthday dinner scene in *Notting Hill.* We all agreed that as long as he was in the room, we just wouldn't acknowledge it. That fragile understanding was like a membrane stretched to its limit, and we were all committed to keeping it intact, come hell or high water.

We rarely even discussed him once he logged out, unless he had done something awkward, like accusing one of us of drinking Snapple just because he, or at least Leo, did. When we did talk about him, we kept those conversations to ourselves, dipping out into private chats rather than bringing it up in the main room. For me, my go-to gossip buddy was always Kim.

Whether it was out of basic courtesy for someone who seemed to crave a low-stakes connection or out of pure self-preservation, we treaded lightly. We all knew one wrong move would ruin it. After all, we never knew when he might pop back in and no one wanted to be the idiot who hit send on an incriminating message at the exact moment he walked through the door.

The second misstep happened late one Friday night, a few weeks later.

By that point in the night, most of the regulars had logged off, leaving just me and Bobby, the emotionally teenaged man in an adult's body. The room felt unusually still with only two of us left and we were both multitasking elsewhere. And then, just as I was debating whether to call it a night myself, a new-chatter notification popped up.

Blungo has entered the chat.

At around 3 a.m., or midnight in Leo's time zone, Blungo came staggering in, clearly inebriated, making a scene as he fumbled his way into the room. If chat rooms had virtual furniture, he would have knocked over a chair and sent a trash can rolling across the floor.

I've spent years trying to make sense of what happened next. Maybe he didn't notice Bobby's name sitting right there in the user list and thought I was alone in the room. Perhaps he had attempted to private message me and mistakenly clicked one too many times. He was probably just too drunk to care, but I'll never forget it.

He started talking in third person.

Leo third person.

"Weeeeeelp, Leo's drunk tonight!" he announced.

Even the text seemed infused with the smell of liquor. I don't remember much of what he said after that, because the moment the words left his keyboard, I kicked into full-on damage control mode.

Bobby was not the person you wanted to flub up in front of. I scrambled to click the private chat button and fired off a message to Blungo.

"*Shhhhhh! Look at what you're doing!!!*"

At least, that's how I remember it. I probably wasn't that blunt, but that's how it lives in my memory.

Blungo clamored for a cover-up.

"Ooooh I just eman hes always parying weekend so," he stammered, a glorious typo salad that read exactly like slurred speech, straight out of the old joke, "I'm not so very drunk, ossifer."

But it was too late. Too, too late.

For once, I was relieved when Blungo logged out just a few minutes later, because Bobby didn't buy it for a second.

I pleaded with him not to say anything, but I could almost hear him hyperventilating through the screen. He hadn't been in the room for the infamous "Snapple Slip," and now, finally, he was getting his moment.

The second Blungo left, Bobby sprinted to LSB and clattered out a frenzied new post, outright begging him to come back to The Cabana.

I didn't even see it until the next morning.

Still mortified from the night before, I logged on only to find Bobby's post sitting there, big, bold, and completely devoid of replies, hovering near the top of the board like a big embarrassing billboard. We had been so careful not to geek out as to not scare Blungo away. I prayed for new posts to flood in, pushing it onto the next page and out of sight before Blungo could see it.

In the moment, it felt like the incident had played out exactly how it should have if Blungo was who we thought he was, not just some bored Milton getting his kicks by toying with Leo's fans. After all, they *do* say that alcohol acts as a truth serum.

I recently came across an interview Leo gave around that time, one I don't remember seeing back then. It was one of those editorial pieces wherein the writer includes behind-the-scenes observations alongside the typical interview Q&A. At one point, Leo announced he needed a nap before continuing and, just like Blungo had done that night, referred to himself in the third person.

I had never considered that this might have been part of a coping mechanism, a phase of projecting himself outward in an effort to make maintaining a guarded public image that didn't necessarily match reality a little less uncomfortable. Or maybe it was simply an attempt at endearing himself that doesn't warrant psychoanalysis at all. But even now, decades later, it's one of those memories that occasionally launches itself into my consciousness like a Pop-Tart from a broken toaster.

SURPRISE! THAT WAS WEIRD, WASN'T IT?!

And I still can't help but wonder… why, oh why, on earth did he have to do *that* specific thing in front of *that* specific person?

I mentally filed it alongside the Snapple Slip, another moment that raised more questions than it answered. On one hand, I could effortlessly picture a sauced-up 24 year old Leo inadvertently revealing his true self. On the other, a fake-Leo might have seen it as the perfect bait, a layered performance designed to keep us guessing. This type of paradox was perhaps articulated best by the magnum opus *Tropic Thunder*: "a dude playing a dude disguised as another dude."

It was all very confusing.

When I sat down to outline this book, memories of various moments with Blungo kept reemerging, as if I were digging through a storage closet full of things I had long forgotten I owned. I kept surprising myself with my ability to retain mundane details of innocuous conversations from so long ago, when I can't even remember my own phone number.

There was the night Blungo dropped into the room when the O Chat refused to connect, mumbling about servers and wondering what they should check to find the problem. When I asked what browser he was using, he responded with, "What's a browser?"

From what I knew of him, Leo was more of a console gamer than a computer nerd, so he could be forgiven for not knowing what a browser was. Still, I always found it amusing he didn't know basic computer lingo even in the technologically advanced year of 1999. "You guys have all these secret codes like LOL, I'm just getting used to it," he said during one of his few official appearances in the O Chat, testifying to his own computing inexperience.

In case you were interested, Blungo was using the browser bundled inside the AOL interface, like a true internet newb.

At one point, the conversation drifted to my job search earlier that year, to which he casually asked, "At least you got unemployment, right?" It was the first time in my young adult life I'd even considered the possibility. *I could have been getting unemployment that whole time? THE WHOLE TIME?!* I scolded myself, thinking of the three months I'd spent selling things on eBay just to afford food. It always made perfect sense to me that someone with a lot of lower-profile actor friends would be well acquainted with that.

But the most bittersweet by far was when he mentioned Paradise Isle… well, sort of. He didn't remember the name, so I'll never know which iteration he saw, but he definitely knew about the site where adult fans wrote erotic fan fiction about Leo.

Better yet, he thought it was cringe, before that was even a thing. And he didn't hold back, briefly mocking some of the writing with the kind of flippant dismissal that made it clear he found the whole thing ludicrous and maybe even a little bit gross.

"Oooooh Leo, touch me *here*," he sarcastically typed.

I blushed behind my monitor.

At least he hadn't realized I had been part of it once, or, much, much worse, that I was the one who started it. That's a fact I've never admitted publicly until now, something I've always felt compelled to apologize for but had been too embarrassed to bring it up at the time.

Still, Blungo had inadvertently given me the closure I didn't even realize I still craved after the whole Paradise Island mutiny. Not only did he think their site was laughable, definitely not somewhere he'd ever spend any real time, but here he was, hanging out with me, the very person they had so cruelly banished.

Who's laughing now, ladies?

Chapter 12: Meating of the Minds

It had been over a year since *The Beach* had been announced as Leonardo DiCaprio's follow-up project to *Titanic,* and the fandom was growing restless. By autumn, everyone was salivating for any scrap of news about Leo's long-awaited return to the big screen. With the film's U.S. release still months away, anticipation was at a fever pitch.

Between June and late September 1999, the official chat room had settled on a Monday-through-Thursday schedule and had hosted dozens of scheduled events, many featuring guests from Leo's personal life. Most of the employees of Birken made regular appearances, but the chatmaster role was most often played by Felix or Jubei. That is, at least as far as we were told.

Back in The Cabana chat room, Kim and I had already floated the idea of seeing *The Beach* for the first time together, but with both of us stuck in our respective cities on opening weekend, it wasn't going to happen. That kindled another idea. Why not help other fans coordinate their own meetups? Without stopping to consider how much work a project like that would take, a new website, "Meet at the Beach," was created.

The concept was as simple as the name. Fans could sign up to find others in their area to have someone to share the experience of opening night with who was just as enthusiastic as they were. I spent my spare time, while of course multitasking in the chat room, organizing small groups and helping people locate their nearest fellow Leo devotees.

The new fan project was a moderate success. We managed to connect a handful of fan groups, some halfway around the world. As Kim and I organized a T-shirt order for participants to wear so they could recognize each other in theaters, Blungo popped into the chat, listening intently to my blathering about my latest fan-brainchild.

At one point, he dropped one of those little memorable nuggets, accidentally misspelling "Meet" as M-E-A-T. He leaned into it with the dry self-awareness one might expect from someone used to being consumed by the public eye.

"Well, that's one hell of a Freudian slip," he quipped.

Blungo had been dropping by The Cabana at random times and on different days of the week all summer. He often showed up during the late-night hours on weekends, unless the celebrity gossip e-zines reported that Leo had traveled from his home in Los Angeles to New York. On those occasions, without a word of explanation on his part and typically hours before Leo's whereabouts were reported by the tabloids, Blungo's visits would mysteriously jump to much earlier in the evening.

It would be a few more months before Leo would embark on the press tour for *The Beach* to provide us with endless new content to discuss. In the meantime, the only events on the horizon were the O Chats. Special guests were becoming more sporadic, and there were none scheduled for the upcoming week, just an expectation that whoever was running the Birken account would be rambling their usual off-topic nonsense.

The initial thrill of the scheduled O Chats had started to fade once fans realized Leo rarely appeared as a special guest. At least, it had for me. Still, his admission that he occasionally silently observed incited a buzz of anticipation among participants, who filled the room with a nervous energy that never seemed to relax, even after weeks of near-daily chats had passed. The O Chat was the closest most fans ever got to chatting with Leo one-on-one, but the regulars of The Cabana knew *our* room was the place to be.

When I logged into the O Chat one September afternoon, I had no reason to believe that day would be any different. I was only half-watching, my attention split between Birken's scattered commentary and another browser window, where The Cabana sat tucked beneath the O Chat.

The Cabana was always empty while the regulars were away at the O Chats. I was the only one who was always in both, unable to let go of the urge to keep my room from going entirely dark whenever

I was at my computer and able to prevent it. I told myself that if someone stopped by who couldn't afford the fan club dues, The Cabana could still offer them a real-time play-by-play.

Just like Leo's website had been, I built The Cabana to accommodate those old monitors that maxed out at an 800×600 resolution, filling the screen edge to edge. Without enough space to arrange them side-by-side, I layered the chats, flipping back and forth between browser windows. It did the job, at least until something in the hidden window unexpectedly needed attention.

When the O Chat moved onto a topic I didn't care much about, I clicked over to The Cabana, only to find Blungo there, alone, trying to get my attention.

"Hey! What's up today?" he asked. "Hellooooo?"

I blinked at the screen. I hadn't even heard the notification when he came in. He always dropped by unannounced, his timing entirely unpredictable.

Then, almost to himself, "Oh, I guess you're in the other room."

"So sorry! I was watching the O Chat and didn't hear you come in," I finally replied.

"Oh really? What's going on in there?"

I filled him in on Birken's usual shenanigans and aimless chatter. There was nothing special to report, just another night of fans trying to get a word in edgewise as the mysterious chatmaster picked topics for discussion that had nothing to do with Leo or his films. Today, the role of Birken was being played by Felix.

"Why don't you ask him what Leo's favorite T-shirt is?" Blungo suggested.

I hesitated. The chatmaster was never going to see it. The question would get swallowed up in seconds, lost in the relentless torrent of fan chatter. Besides, I wasn't the type to spam the chat with questions begging for attention. I had more pride than that.

Felix was already knee-deep in one of his usual non-Leo-related tangents, anyway. He preferred to treat the entire chat room like a private discussion, fixating on a topic and responding to whomever he happened to see answer his questions as if he were conversing with one person. If your post wasn't on topic, you were just shouting into a black hole.

"I don't think he'll see it. It's moving too fast," I replied, hoping that would be the end of it.

"Just *ask* him," Blungo pushed.

I sighed, my fingers hovering over the keyboard. Seriously? Of all the questions, *this* was the one? There were so many better options, deeper, more thought provoking, more likely to warrant an answer or spawn an intriguing discussion, but fine. Blungo gets what Blungo wants.

With a begrudging sense of duty, I typed it out and waited before hitting the Enter key. My eyes stayed glued to the screen, tracking Felix's every move, ready to jump in the moment he posted his next question. Timing was everything. If I sent it while he was typing, it would be instantly lost to the scroll, buried under a flood of other messages. But if I could slip it in right after he hit enter when he would be searching the chat for a response, there was a small chance he'd manage to see it before it raced off the screen.

I hit enter and watched as my message disappeared up and off the chat window almost instantly.

Yup. There it goes, flying off into the ether, I thought to myself.

I waited for a beat, just in case. Just in case Felix somehow caught it in the madness, just in case he acknowledged it, just in case he responded.

Nothing.

There was no pause and no flicker of recognition. There hadn't been even the slightest hint that he had seen it. The chat rolled on, undeterred, and my question was just another whisper lost in the noise.

A minute passed. Then another.

Felix continued his conversation, none the wiser. The moment had long passed and taken any hope of an answer with it.

I switched back to The Cabana. "It's really busy in there today," I started to explain.

"What did he say?" Blungo asked.

"He never answered, it's just going too fast," I repeated.

"Give me a minute," Blungo said, before falling silent.

I clicked back over to the O Chat, wondering if he actually had something up his sleeve.

At least a full five minutes had passed since the question had zipped off the screen, and Felix was still babbling about whatever off-the-wall topic someone had thrown out before I had even found Blungo in The Cabana in the first place. There was no way he'd seen it. He never would have gone digging for it while mid-conversation. If he had even wanted to try, he'd never have found it. That's why what happened next was so astonishing.

Stopping the conversation momentarily to drop in a very awkwardly wedged-in comment, Felix typed,

"Leo's favorite T-shirt is…"

I don't even remember what he said it was. It was one of those moments in movies when everything goes mute and all you can hear is that high-pitched ringing as if an explosive has just gone off next to your head.

When my brain finally rebooted, all I could think was:

OH.

MY.

GOD.

Chapter 13: When Leo Logged Off

I only ever told one person in my real life about Blungo. I knew it sounded unbelievable, and I knew that not being able to prove what I experienced that day would make me seem hopelessly pathetic. But honestly, I'm not sure having proof would've been any better. Bragging about it likely would've just made me sound pretentious. It didn't make me special by association. I didn't have delusions that we had some kind of bond. It just… was what it was.

It was too preposterous to be real, yet too perfectly timed to be faked. Even now, I sometimes question it myself. Then I replay that day's chat in my head, stacking up all the supporting evidence from the weeks leading up to it, reassuring myself that I hadn't just imagined it.

When I finally shared the story with Brenda, I thought she'd get it. She had been there from the beginning, watching my online world take shape, seeing how deeply I had embedded myself into this strange little digital universe. If anyone would understand, it was her. Or so I thought.

Her response wasn't curiosity or even cautious skepticism. It was a general apathy laced with hints of politely concealed disbelief. I realized then that I was never going to be able to talk to anyone about it. If even Brenda, the one person who had witnessed my online world unfold from the very beginning, didn't really believe me, no one would.

"We need to get you out of that apartment and out of that fantasy world you're in," she said.

I had only told my truth, laid out the facts as I knew them, and perhaps engaged in a little wishful thinking, but she seemed convinced I'd lost myself in a fool's paradise. It stung more than I expected.

Okay. Yeah. I got it. I was a young, working-class chubby girl with average looks. I was introverted, barely making ends meet in an entry-level office job with no prestige, and living alone in a tiny cheap apartment in a part of Tennessee the rest of the country barely noticed. One simply doesn't get much more invisible than that. Who could possibly believe I'd been casually chatting with arguably the most famous actor of our generation? Even I think it sounds like something a deranged fan would dream up, some manic grasp at proximity to a star who would never even know they were alive. From her perspective, it must have seemed downright pitiful.

The only famous person I'd ever met until then was, fittingly, given the nerd factor of my future career, Marina Sirtis from *Star Trek: The Next Generation.* Jo Ann took me to a tiny *Star Trek* convention in the early '90s, where Marina was the sole guest.

The setup was perfectly efficient, with rows of chairs arranged for her Q&A audience doubling as a switchback queue beforehand, offering built-in seating so fans could rest their feet whenever the line paused. It had the distinct feeling of a game of mass-Musical Chairs.

As I snaked my way between the rows of chairs, I had plenty of time to watch Marina interact with fans from different angles, taking in every detail of how she engaged with each person. I could feel the energy pulsing through the crowd, a collective excitement that only grew stronger the closer I got. My nerves ramped up with each step forward, but I kept my composure right up until I reached the table to choose a photo for her to sign. Then, without warning, something odd happened to me.

When we finally reached the table where she was seated, all I remember feeling was… embarrassed. The excitement that had carried me through the line dissipated the moment I was face to face with her. I didn't say anything, not even my name for the autograph. Instead, an overwhelming urge to apologize for bothering her overtook me, and I just silently slid the photograph across the table, collected the signature, nodded a quiet "thank you," and walked away.

Somewhere in that moment, it hit me. I didn't actually care about the autograph itself. I had stood in line, paid my money, and waited my turn, but now that I was here, it all felt unnervingly superficial. I suddenly felt foolish for having gone through the motions, as if I'd been playing a part in a ritual at a church I didn't belong to.

I had watched this woman on my television for years. *Star Trek: The Next Generation* was one of my favorite shows, and her character was the love interest of my favorite bearded first officer, a role played by Jonathan Frakes, a former (albeit very brief) celebrity crush of mine.

The show had carried me through those rough few months of my first attempt at independence before moving back home, when I could afford no other form of entertainment but grainy over-the-air television. But standing in front of her, all of that faded into the background.

In that moment, she wasn't a larger-than-life figure or someone I'd spent years admiring from afar. She was just another person sitting there doing her job, a human being who, at the end of the day, ate, slept, and farted like the rest of us. No more or less special in the grand scheme of things than any other animal on earth, including me. I had been excited to see what she was like in person, but once I did, I realized the only difference between us was how high others had placed our pedestals.

But back in present-day 1999, I was shook.

Blungo had just proven, beyond a shadow of a doubt, that even if he wasn't who we thought he was, he was at least in contact with the chatmaster of the official chat room on the official website of one Leonardo Wilhelm DiCaprio.

I sat there in stunned silence trying to come up with some kind of calm, breezy response as if it hadn't just rocked my world. The only thing I could pull from my brain was…

"Smart Alec."

Gaaaaahdammit, I grumbled at myself.

Not that Blungo would ever remember the misspelling had he even noticed it, but it's become one of those pesky intrusive thoughts that taunt me on sleepless nights, surfacing just as I'm beginning to nod off. I caught it in real time but didn't bother correcting it. I was too busy trying and failing to appear unfazed.

For the record, it's A-L-E-C-*K*. There, now I can sleep.

"I like to be in control," Blungo wryly replied.

Over the years, I've noticed in interviews that actors often talk about feeling burdened by their lack of control during the production process. They're shuffled around, directed on every movement, told where to go, what to say, and how to stand. Insurance policies dictate their off-camera behavior mid-project, and they're often locked into strict diets or grueling fitness routines just to maintain a specific look for a role. It's a bizarre contradiction, being the face of a movie, yet having so little agency over their own day-to-day routines during the making of films.

Leo, in particular, hadn't only just emerged from filming a new project, but also the onslaught of Leomania. It wasn't just life in a fishbowl, like any average celebrity. It must have felt like living under a high-powered microscope, like having thousands of stalkers all at once. No other actor, before or since, has drawn the same level of global, sustained hysteria as Leo did in the post-*Titanic* years.

We'd all heard the stories of the constant surveillance by paparazzi, the impossibility of going *anywhere* without causing a scene, and even getting chased by fans through the Louvre. It must have been exhausting. So, while I wasn't exactly delighted about being toyed with, I got it. I understood, at least as much as a little anony-mouse from the masses possibly could. He just needed to seize control wherever he could find it.

"Okay, well, I just dropped in for a few minutes, I've got to run," he said, cutting the interaction short just as my mind was reeling.

"You're going to drop this bomb on me and then leave?!" I blurted, failing miserably at my attempt to appear indifferent.

"What *bomb*?" he replied.

What *bomb*, he says. What do you mean, *what bomb*?

Such a simple question, yet it violently shoved me into his perspective. Of course, it wasn't a big deal to *him*. Duh. Besides, it wasn't as if he hadn't been dropping clues the entire time.

I don't remember how I tried to recover, but I know I clumsily tried to play it off, wishing him well for the rest of his evening. At least there was Kim. She'd help me process what had just happened. And more importantly, I knew she'd believe me.

I could never claim it was irrefutable proof that Blungo was Leo, though I will always believe it was. I will also always believe that he *meant* for that interaction to serve as my own personal proof of it, though it appeared he fully believed I already had no doubt who he was by then. After all that time getting to know all of us, I can only assume that he wanted *someone* to know who he really was. I had earned his trust from that first night when I posted the room rules to protect him. He knew I was the one with the admin login who could be his virtual bodyguard. It was only natural that he chose me.

The trouble is, my logic-driven brain will never stop questioning it. I never saw his face. I never heard his voice. And no matter how much I believe it, it isn't something I can ever truly, fully verify.

The timing of that incident left me, at least, with little doubt that if Blungo wasn't Leo, then he was at least someone within his orbit. The delay in receiving a response to my question could only mean one thing. He had called Felix, whoever "Felix" was, and instructed him to answer the question.

That was the only explanation that made sense. Otherwise, how would the chatmaster have known to answer that specific question out of the dozens that flew by after I posted it? Why pause the conversation to respond to a single off-topic question at all? The simplest answer was that Blungo had told him to. And that meant Blungo was, at the very least, part of Leo's inner circle.

So, whether it was Leo himself or someone close enough to have Felix on speed dial, my *neener neener boo boo* to Paradise Isle still stands.

Court adjourned.

Thankfully, it hadn't been a dramatic final reveal before vaporizing forever in a cloud of smoke. The next time I saw Blungo was during the following O Chat, once again with me juggling two windows, flipping between rooms. And once again, I completely missed his entrance into The Cabana.

"Hellooooooo, you're going to leave *the man* here alone?" he teased, clearly poking fun at our last interaction.

That was it. That was the *only* time he ever directly insinuated (on purpose, while sober) that he was Leo, after already handing me proof that he was at least connected to him.

Looking back, I suppose I should've known these were some of the last days I'd have with Blungo. Leo would soon be busily preparing for the premiere of *The Beach* and on top of that, trouble was brewing in Thailand. A controversy over the film's production had been simmering for months, with environmental groups and local activists raising concerns about the damage caused to the filming location. The press was beginning to catch wind of it, and it was only a matter of time before Leo himself would be dragged into the storm.

I didn't realize it then, but the tides were already shifting.

One day, I got an email from Richard, the teacher at the school in Thailand. He sounded rattled. Protests had broken out in the streets and had begun to escalate, with activists wearing masks of Leo's face to make their point. The controversy centered around how the government had allowed filming on Ko Phi Phi Leh Island, part of a protected national park. The production had altered the natural landscape, flattening sand dunes and clearing vegetation, to make the beach look more "perfect." Now, the fallout was ruthless.

Despite 20th Century Fox's efforts to restore the island and their removal of tons of trash that was there before they arrived, the damage had sparked lawsuits that would drag through Thai courts for nearly two decades. And at the center of it all, one man… Leo.

Whether he had personally made any decisions or not, his name was the one making headlines.

Richard knew about my Meet at the Beach project and was worried I might catch some blowback from activists. He wanted to give me a heads-up before the story made its way into American news outlets. It was a considerate warning, and for a moment, I panicked, wondering if my little fan project might somehow get tangled in something much bigger than I'd ever intended.

My overactive imagination dreamed up angry emails flooding my inbox, protestors somehow finding a way to spin my dinky little website into part of the controversy, or worse, getting targeted by media looking for an original angle on the story. But, as it turned out, my fears were unfounded. The protests stayed focused on the real issue: the environmental damage and the government's role in it. Meet at the Beach, thankfully, remained entirely under the radar.

Leo has always been known as an environmentalist. He served as the chairman and host of Earth Day 2000 on the National Mall in Washington, D.C. just two months after *The Beach* opened in theaters. LSB even sent a good-sized contingent of fans to see his speech in person. I knew being attached to a project embroiled in environmental controversy, especially with protesters literally using his face, had to weigh heavily on him. It wasn't just bad press, it was personal. So, the next time I saw Blungo in The Cabana, I sent him a private message.

"I heard about the protests over the island. Are you okay?"

"Who told you?! Was it Sarah?" he snapped.

To this day, I still have no idea who "Sarah" was.

At first, I matched his earlier cheek with a vague, "Oh, people just like to tell me things." He was in no mood for my games, so I hurriedly clarified that it was Richard, but that only confused him. He thought I meant the character from *The Beach*.

"No, no. The teacher from the school that runs the Thai Kids' site," I explained.

That seemed to satisfy him, but that knee-jerk paranoia has always made me wonder, who was *Sarah*, and why was his first assumption that she had talked to me? More than anything, I didn't want him blaming her, whoever she was, for something she didn't do.

If that wasn't our last chat, then the true final one must have been so unremarkable that my mind never saw fit to store it, because this is the last interaction I can recall. Late one night, after I'd already gone to bed, Blungo popped into the chat room where the other regulars were still hanging out. He asked them to let me know he'd be gone for a while. He provided no explanations and no timelines, just that he'd be… gone.

The next day, tabloid headlines confirmed that Leo had been spotted rushing toward a departure gate at LAX. I'll never know where he was headed, except to say that he flew out of our lives that day as abruptly as he had entered.

Chapter 14: Millennium Metamorphosis

I had a minor quarter-life crisis when I turned 25 in the summer of 1999, afraid I was letting my precious youth slip through my fingers. I wasn't unhappy, but it felt like I was supposed to be having more fun than I was. I often blamed my post-high school weight gain for my lack of friends, convinced that if I were thinner, I'd be more confident, more likable… more *something.*

I always joked that I had the metabolic rate of a dying elephant, courtesy of my father's side of the family who were all supersized. My mother's family wasn't particularly heavy, but my grandmother had raised her daughters with a Great Depression-era understanding of lard that only a new mother in the 1930s could possess. I was never going to be skinny, and I would spend a lifetime fighting, and usually failing, not to be thick.

The underlying truth was, I had no idea how socially awkward I really was and blaming it on my size wasn't helping. I only knew that making friends never seemed to come easily, and every so often, a misguided but well-intentioned bystander would inform me that someone had been gossiping that I was "annoying." I didn't have the self-awareness to know why when I was younger, and that uncertainty bothered me more than the insult itself.

That sort of thing began happening in early childhood, when the high expectations of my first day of kindergarten ended in the harsh crash of reality. I had imagined making immediate friends, laughing as we played together on the swings, maybe even being invited to share crayons at craft time. Instead, I spent all of recess that first day sitting alone on a bench, watching the other girls pair up and skip off hand in hand. I didn't understand why I wasn't included, why no one had turned to me with an expectant "*Come on!*" It wouldn't be the last time I cried myself to sleep, sobbing into my pillow as my flustered mother tried to console me.

"No one lo-o-oooves me," I remember howling through the flood of tears streaming down my little face.

I was almost 50 before I realized that perhaps I wasn't typical, socially speaking. Shallow as it can be, social media can serve as a kind of mirror, its algorithms filling your feeds with like-minded people who reflect things back at you that you hadn't recognized before. Memories came flooding back of clumsily attempting to connect with others through making observational comments that I believed would be funny or relatable, but instead came across as off-putting or even tactless. I told myself I was just using humor as a defense mechanism and that everyone knew I was just doing my "Chandler" bit, but I already knew that wasn't true.

Those experiences chipped away at my confidence from that tender age forward, shaping how I navigate the world and how the world reacts to me navigating in it. Small talk and pleasantries have always felt foreign and disingenuous to me, like fudging through a language I never really learned.

It never occurs to me to ask someone how their day is, because I assume everyone secretly finds that question just as tedious as I do. The expected answer is always something polite, making the whole exchange feel more like a mindless habit than a genuine interaction. Why ask if no one really wants the truth? The social script has already been written: *Good, how about you?* I've never understood the point of reciting lines that don't mean anything.

It was never that I cared what people thought of me, at least not primarily. I just hated dealing with the fallout of their negative reactions, so I avoided people altogether, though I didn't realize that was the reason. I was at least self-aware enough to see that I was the only one in the room who seemed to evoke those responses, and I often wrestled privately with why I was different or how to change it.

It has always felt like being a baby chick getting pecked to death by its siblings for being so subtly different that even I wasn't sure what the difference was. The imbalance fed a repressed but constant disillusionment that surfaced only as vague, confusing frustration.

By 25, I thought I was ready to shed my emotional armor, even if I still didn't understand why I had needed it. I'd spent years retreating inward, trying to either avoid the fatigue of social interaction or lying in bed suffering from it, but something had changed. Maybe I was just done feeling invisible. Maybe I was finally ready to take advantage of my youth before it left me. Whatever it was, it gave me the push I needed to start getting in shape.

I'd been quietly dropping pounds as a sort of side-quest to the whole Blungo experience, and once he vanished before the release of *The Beach*, I was ready to emerge as a brand-new butterfly. With a renewed sense of confidence and the rise of online dating opening up new possibilities, the timing felt perfect. I was young, single, and for the first time in my life, I truly felt beautiful. More than that, I was ready for the world to see it and began regularly going on dates.

As I was transforming physically, so was the media office where I spent my days. By the end of my first month of employment there, the office manager and the payroll clerk left for other jobs. The turnover created an uncertain, unsettled atmosphere, with everyone waiting to see who would step in to fill the gaps. I just focused on my work and waited.

One afternoon, I overheard the district manager interviewing a candidate named Valerie for the office manager position. Her voice carried a light, higher-pitched lilt, with an almost timid quality. She didn't strike me as the kind of animated, fun personality I had secretly hoped for, someone who could inject some energy into our often dull and uneventful office. She seemed polite and professional, perfectly capable for the role, but I doubted she was someone I would genuinely connect with.

I secretly hoped she wouldn't get the job.

She did, and I was wrong.

Valerie turned out to be more of a confidante and mentor than a boss. She was warm, easygoing, and had the kind of dry humor that made me feel instantly comfortable. Instead of the buttoned-up, serious manager I had expected, she was surprisingly fun and very empathetic. For someone only a few years older than me, she was far more mature and professional than I was at the time. Working with me must've felt like standing next to a whirling dervish to someone with such a calm countenance. The restless energy I had in my youth paired with my odd sense of humor could be a lot to take, but we counterbalanced each other nicely.

While we generally respected the boundaries of our working relationship, we occasionally scheduled a "business lunch," which was code for slipping away from the office for a quick gossip sesh, just the two of us. I loved making her laugh, and for a while, I treated it as a job requirement. Eventually, though, she had to ask me to stop jumping out and scaring her, because, as it turned out, that was *nervous* laughter.

Y2K was rapidly approaching, preceded by a wave of paranoia about economic collapse and the catastrophic ruin of anything that relied on computers. People genuinely feared that computerized cars, banking systems, gas pumps, cash registers, and even automatic grocery store doors would grind to a halt at the stroke of midnight. The fear stemmed from the belief that systems that stored years as two digits instead of four would mistakenly think it was 1900 instead of 2000, throwing everything into turmoil.

At the media office, my temp job had evolved into a full-time direct hire position, and with that promotion came a new title. I was now the local office IT liaison. My "proficiency," which mostly boiled down to knowing how to share files between the office computers, had apparently set me apart. It was enough to impress my coworkers, but when a corporate IT tech arrived to install a new piece of equipment and spotted the custom company-branded desktop wallpaper I had made, she sneered and declared that I "only knew enough to get myself in trouble."

And now, just in time for the prophesied Computer Apocalypse, I was being volun*told* for my most critical mission yet.

Headquarters had decreed that someone had to be onsite early on the morning of January 1st to verify that the Y2K patches had worked, ensuring the office didn't descend into technological ruin. Naturally, that person was going to be me. Never mind that my IT troubleshooting ability at the time barely extended beyond "turn it off and back on again." If the world was truly going to collapse into digital lawlessness, at least I'd have a front-row seat to watch it all go up in flames.

"I'll make it worth your while," the district manager promised, though she never specified how. I forced a smile, pretending to be excited about putting my computer skills to use in a real, official capacity, but inside, I was screaming. A new millennium celebration only comes around once every 40 generations. This wasn't just once in a lifetime, it was once in dozens of lifetimes. And I was going to spend it in a dimly lit office, staring at a computer screen, waiting to see if the world collapsed.

I had already planned to ring in the New Year with Kim at her lake house, and with the news that I would now have to be in Knoxville early the next day, she graciously promised to be my personal alarm clock. It was a kind gesture, but it didn't fully soften the blow. I wanted to toast the new millennium at midnight and sit up all night Cold Ducking with Kim without constantly glancing at the clock or worrying about a hangover.

Instead, I'd be waking up at the crack of dawn, driving bleary-eyed back into town, and spending the first hours of the 21st century alone in a dusty office on the bad side of town, watching computers reboot and hoping nothing crashed so I could get the hell out of there as expeditiously as possible.

When the day came, everything was fine, of course, until the next payday hit and no one got paid. Turns out, I had diligently patched the Windows computers but had completely overlooked the payroll terminal, the one machine in the place that mattered most and was the most likely to fail, given its age. The oversight was promptly remedied, but it didn't go unnoticed. In hindsight, that little snafu might have been why the manager's vague promise of making it "worth my while" never materialized. I didn't even get paid for the hours I worked that day. At least I had "IT Support Liaison" to put on my résumé, either way.

As I came into my own professionally, I was also wrapping up my glow-up personally. I had lost 100 pounds, but still felt like I needed a little polish to look my best. I started leaving the office during lunch for some quick tanning sessions, which I'm now relieved to say was a brief addiction to tanning beds since spray tans of the day were still a poor, unnatural-looking substitute.

When the district manager complained about my new lunchtime hobby, Valerie came to my defense. "I can't tell her what she can and can't do on her own lunch hour," she reportedly told her. Val also reminded me of the time the same manager had been irritated when I arrived at work with hair that was still wet from my morning shower. I could concede that point. It wasn't terribly professional despite ours not being a public-facing office, but she did seem to enjoy nitpicking everything I did.

Valerie wasn't just supportive, she was protective. "You need to watch out for her," she warned. Thanks to Sharon back at the appliance call center, I was used to managers who had it out for me for personal reasons.

I will always credit Valerie with helping me transition from an unprofessional and often obnoxious kid into a fully formed adult, though she never knew she had that effect on me, especially since her influence didn't get to last very long.

Before the year was out, she accepted a new job with another company and recommended me as her replacement in the office manager role.

Chapter 15: The Summer of Sooz

As much as I enjoyed the artistic outlet of creating websites and would've loved to make a living at it, I couldn't see myself channeling it into a full-time job. After all, I wasn't properly trained, and there was still so much I didn't know about web design. I still relied heavily on online graphics generators, had zero experience with high-end editing software, and knew absolutely nothing about managing enterprise-level websites.

At the end of the day, I knew fan sites weren't going to provide the foundation for a career, especially not in Y2K, when seemingly everyone with an internet connection had a GeoCities or Angelfire homepage and at least a passing knowledge of basic HTML. Within a few more years, platforms like MySpace would make those skills even more mainstream as users learned to code in order to customize their social media profiles. My abilities were beginner-level at best, no matter how advanced I liked to believe they were. That was fine for personal websites but not corporate America.

Instead of chasing some far-fetched dream of a career in web design, I used my self-described expertise to craft a brand-new homepage for myself, an elaborate display of my various creative pursuits. Terribly mixed MP3s of cover songs, recorded using cheap karaoke tracks and my mediocre singing voice, took center page. It was a talent I'd once believed was top-tier thanks to my senior year in high school as the unofficial lead soprano in my school's mixed choir.

That title, unofficial or not, had led me to peacocking all over campus, perfectly embodying the school's stereotype of the "pretentious choir snob." It didn't help that our choir director pulled me and the likewise-unofficial lead tenor aside to tell us we'd be playing the leads when he planned a spring production of *West Side Story*.

Naturally, we both thought, *Of course we are.*

We still had to sit through the motions of sham auditions, staged to appease the hopeful parents of other kids, but we'd been assured the roles were ours, so long as we kept it on the down low. I accidentally blew the cover 10 years later at a reunion, when the other girls were reminiscing about their auditions for Maria.

"There were *auditions*?" I said, stupidly surprised. "I don't remember auditioning."

What I did remember, in intense detail, was the fear of being frozen by stage fright, a debilitating dread that set in even before our first rehearsal. I could sing in front of audiences packed with strangers with more confidence than I had a right to claim, but ask me to *speak* and I'd seize up like an engine running dry of oil. Fortunately, the musical was scrapped in favor of a senior trip to perform at a festival in Miami. Still, everyone had known I'd been cast. Now they knew their auditions had been a farce.

I never wanted to admit I was one of those girls who peaked in high school, still bragging years later that I'd been "featured in several solos and was the only girl from my school that year to make All-State." As sad as that may have been, the experience gave me just enough confidence to exist in the real world, so I hung onto it, stretching its impact much farther into adulthood than I probably should have.

Our production of *West Side Story* would've undoubtedly been an unmitigated disaster, but just being cast as the lead made me feel like part of an elite club of vocalists, on par with any seasoned Broadway veteran. I had no concept at all of the years of theatrical, dance, and vocal training those performers endure, or the grueling audition seasons and countless rejections they face to get their names in lights. No, I figured my only problem was that I just hadn't been discovered yet. Maybe a website would help.

Eight years removed from that tiny spotlight, I was still coasting on the memory, blissfully unaware that my vocal prowess had never been as impressive as I'd believed. Everyone who knew me knew I was an "aspiring singer," though I never auditioned or performed. When *American Idol* debuted, friends routinely told me I should audition, but I just scoffed and said I was over the age limit. At least it was the truth. When the show first aired, I was already beyond the original cutoff, and by the time they raised the limit I was over that age, too. It was the perfect excuse. I knew I'd never make it past the first round.

Within a decade, social media platforms would be bursting with unknown singers whose flawless tone and technique humbled any notion I had of special talent. These days I'm able to admit to myself that I could never compete, but in Y2K, I still fancied myself an undiscovered virtuoso. I just always inherently knew it would never amount to anything, even if that had been true.

I had come to see a more grounded path for myself professionally, somewhere in middle management as the no-nonsense "office boss lady," tapping away at my keyboard while peering over the top of my reading glasses, watching my staff's antics with a mix of amusement and restrained annoyance. I dreamed of a future where I never had to deal with the public directly because I had *people* for that.

With Valerie's support and mentorship, I was progressing rapidly up the management track to reach that goal, gaining confidence in my ability to run an office. The district manager, however, wasn't quite as convinced. As I packed up my desk toys and prepared to move into the now-vacant manager's office, she gave me one final instruction. It was one that felt less like guidance and more like a scolding parent. Never let her catch me with the door closed.

I'm still not entirely sure what she thought I'd do in there.

While my work life was evolving, halfway across the world, the kids who ran the Thai Kids' site were having the best year ever after *The Beach* was released. They had already earned a place of honor in Leo's fan community, but in Y2K, they truly made out like bandits.

As a thank-you for letting us piggyback on their message boards to promote Meet at the Beach, Kim and I sent them a package of our custom T-shirts. A few weeks later, we received a heartwarming photo of all the kids crowded around their instructor, Richard Bradley, beaming with pride as they showed off their bright blue shirts. The Meet at the Beach logo, which I had designed myself, was emblazoned across their chests in black screen printing. It was amazing seeing something I had created worn by kids halfway across the world, one of those rare moments where my online life materialized into something real and tangible.

Those shirts weren't the last surprise waiting for the kids. Just after *The Beach* was released, Birken sent a large care package to the school, filled with promotional goodies similar to the ones offered to Leo's official fan club members. There was some brief drama when an unknown item in the shipment got flagged at customs, delaying its delivery, though I never found out what the suspicious object was. The package, whether still stranded in some airport or safely in the hands of the kids, carried a message even before it arrived. Leo had known about their website.

More importantly, that meant he had known about their message board, the very same board where my chat room had been advertised and where Blungo had found us. I filed it away as another piece of evidence, one more clue that seemed to confirm what I already believed: Blungo wasn't just connected to Leo, Blungo *was* Leo.

Shortly after the movie was released, I stumbled upon another piece of the puzzle tucked inside a quote from one of Leo's press tour interviews for *The Beach*. He briefly spoke candidly about how addictive online interactions could be, and how he eventually had to pull away from them. To the rest of the world, it probably sounded like a passing observation about his character's early reliance on technology. But to me, it felt like watching a friend silently walk away.

I remembered that interview comment as clearly as if I had read it yesterday, because it broke my heart. It wasn't just validation that Leo had spent time online engaging with fans personally, it was confirmation that he had felt drawn to it, maybe even trapped by it. And, though he said he'd be back, if Blungo was indeed Leo, it meant I would never see him again.

The Cabana chat room had served its purpose. It had been a safe haven during a turbulent time in my life, a welcome distraction when I needed one. It gave me friendships, laughter, and something to look forward to when the rest of my world felt uncertain. But as the months passed, the urgency to log in every night faded.

My life was realigning, and the chat room, once my primary escape, was no longer the center of my universe. I had strapped it into the backseat as I sped off into a new career, one that was finally leading somewhere, while I dipped my toes into the dating scene. At long last, I was getting one of those things people always talk about having… a life.

Once the O Chat was shuttered in late September 1999 as Leo's "summer off" came to a close, the other fans' enthusiasm for chatting also began to wane. One by one, the regulars of The Cabana chat room slowly drifted away, their visits becoming less frequent until, eventually, they stopped showing up altogether. There were no dramatic goodbyes, no official closing announcement, just a gradual fading of something that had once felt like a lifeline. Without anyone left to sit in the room keeping the conversation going, I knew it was time to let it go. Before the end of 2000, I shut down the site, closed that chapter of my life, and moved on.

I had barely settled into a new, less-online daily routine when Angie came crashing back into my life in the late spring of 2001. She needed a place to stay after the end of a tumultuous relationship, and moved into the spare bedroom that had once been the center of operations for The Cabana.

With Angie's help, I gradually became a semi-regular of The Old City's nightlife in downtown Knoxville. By summer, the techno dance club Fiction had become my favorite haunt. The place gave off the illusion of a trendy Los Angeles nightclub, the kind where I imagined I might glance over and see Leo lounging in a booth, surrounded by his posse. It provided the stage on which I could play out the fantasy of being the sort of magnetic young woman he might pick out of the crowd from across the club.

Fiction was the place to be if you wanted to feel like you had a seat at the cool kids' table. If the 3 a.m. closing time came too soon and you were bold enough for it, you could head downstairs to The Boiler Room, an underground after-party that ran on BYOB rules thanks to local liquor laws prohibiting alcohol sales after 3 a.m. The party pulsed on until 6 a.m., when glassy-eyed revelers would spill out onto West Jackson Avenue just as dawn began to break. It was a short-lived clubbing obsession that disappeared from my life as quickly as Angie did, the moment she moved back into her parents' little bungalow at the end of September.

That summer etched itself into my memory as my one season of sowing wild oats, a brief interlude of debauchery before returning to the business of adult life. It had also been the summer the world changed when four planes crashed and two towers fell. The juxtaposition of those two realities left me reeling with thoughts of my own mortality.

That was the last summer I visited with Kim at her lake house for a hot Tennessee afternoon get-together. She greeted me with wide eyes, shocked by my weight loss, and her son's jaw nearly hit the floor. "*Wooooooow*," he said in genuine surprise with eyes as wide as quarters. Had they not been expecting me, I'm not sure he would've recognized me.

We settled onto the porch overlooking the sun-dappled water, a bottle of chilled Cold Duck between us, savoring the familiar ritual that had once felt like it would go on forever. The conversation flowed from catching up on each other's lives to lighthearted reminiscing about our old friends from The Cabana, our usual dance of easy camaraderie. But then, as if waiting for the right moment, Kim leaned in with a knowing grin and told me she had another secret.

Always the Gatekeeper.

During the last days of the O Chats, one of the women on LSB had spearheaded a collage project, gathering photos of the regulars from the message boards and arranging them into a framed display to send to Birken, Leo's production company. It could have easily been lost in the mountains of fan mail he received daily, but the collage designer somehow managed to secure direct contact information and successfully sent it off.

In a following O Chat, Birken confirmed that it had safely arrived and was now proudly hanging in their office. The thought was surreal. Our faces, our little online community, framed on a wall where Leo himself would regularly walk past it.

I had contributed a black-and-white photo of myself, one taken during a hilariously chaotic, alcohol-fueled, less-than-amateur photo shoot at a former coworker's apartment. He had climbed onto a chair to snap the shot from above, practically looking straight down my cleavage and maniacally giggling the entire time. By some miracle, the end result was one of the best pictures I had of myself.

Back on the lake house porch, Kim hesitated for a moment, basking in the tension before dropping her real bombshell.

She had managed to get hold of that same secret contact information, the direct line to Birken. She hadn't just tucked it away for safekeeping in case some urgent need arose, she had used it. Not only had she written to them, but she had also received a response.

I sat up straighter, waiting for her to elaborate… but she didn't.

She refused to say what she had written, what they had said in return, or even who had replied. It was infuriating, but also, so perfectly Kim.

A knot of unease formed in my stomach as a new worry crept in. Had she written to ask about Blungo? The thought sent my heart racing. I hadn't wanted him to know I had spoken about him to the others, even if, in hindsight, it shouldn't have mattered.

From the very beginning, the other chat regulars had been far more insistent than I was, convinced that Blungo was Leo. It wasn't a secret, not really. And yet, I had always felt it was my responsibility to keep it quiet, to protect whatever fragile trust had formed, especially after that T-shirt question.

He knew there were moments he hadn't been careful, so much so that, whenever I flip through the scrapbook in my mind, I can't help but be amused at the possibility that someone who is now an Oscar winner didn't have the acting chops to fool us.

But then again, I suppose he wasn't exactly on the clock.

Kim and I had often discussed how to ensure his comfort during his stays in our little fellowship, agreeing that he should never glimpse the sometimes-frantic paddling beneath the surface of our otherwise graceful swan. He should be able to enjoy the safe space we built for him, free of pressure or expectation, unaware of what it took to maintain. So, I had assumed she must've had some other mysterious reason for reaching out to Birken, something entirely unrelated. It must've been something she deemed important enough to keep secret, even from me. I happily believed that self-deception for an entire quarter-century.

As I revisited these memories while planning this book, I finally accepted the truth.

Kim's last word on the matter had already said everything I needed to know about her motive in writing that letter. She hadn't reached out for some official business matter, to warn them of some sinister goings-on in the fandom, nor any of the other explanations my imagination had drummed up.

She *had* been searching for confirmation about Blungo.

"I can't tell you what they said," she finally admitted, "but if you *weren't* talking to *him*, you were definitely talking to one of his friends."

And with that, my dossier of evidence was complete.

Chapter 16: A New WAN and Only

Sensing an opportunity in my newfound confidence, Kim decided it was time to play matchmaker. She told me about a man from her office who, in her words, would be "just my brand of nerd." She was so certain of it that she insisted she be allowed to pass along my email address to him, despite my polite protests.

Flattered but skeptical, I agreed, though I barely gave it a passing thought. I wasn't actively looking for a relationship, at least not a long-distance one, and besides, although I would grow to resent being perceived in later years, I was still enjoying the positive attention my new body attracted. Once a few months passed with no email from my mystery match, the whole conversation faded from my mind entirely.

Then, in November 2001, an email arrived from my ex-husband, Gary. My stomach dropped in instant confusion. Why was *he* reaching out? We hadn't spoken in years, and back then he couldn't even understand what the internet was, much less have an email account. But here he was, nonchalantly mentioning that he had visited my site, downloaded some of my songs, and thought my voice was impressive.

That didn't track. He couldn't have cared less about my hobbies when we were married, so why the sudden interest now?

Wait… how would he have even found my email address? Did he even know what email was? And why was he contacting me at all when our divorce was already final? Why was he acting like we were buddies?

The last time I spoke to my ex-husband was over the phone more than two years earlier, just before I moved into the new apartment.

The day of our breakup, as he packed his things to leave, he assured me he would help me stay afloat until everything was finalized. We had parted on exceptionally civilized and amicable terms, or so I had thought. He knew the rent check had already been mailed, and knew the account would be upside-down if his paycheck wasn't deposited. But once his father got him alone, he convinced him to cut me off without warning.

That phone call had been my last attempt at reaching him, both literally and emotionally. I had wanted to give him the benefit of the doubt, to believe he hadn't intentionally stranded me with no way to pay the bills. If I was wrong, perhaps hearing my voice again would remind him of the promise he made.

I had already begun to realize he wasn't the person I had believed him to be. To protect myself, I put a block on long-distance calls from our landline, just in case he decided to let himself back into our apartment when I wasn't home and rack up an expensive bill on his way out. I didn't know what he was capable of anymore, and

I wasn't taking any chances. So, when the rent check bounced and I needed to call him at his parent's house in Murfreesboro to find out what he planned to do about it, I had to use Brenda's phone.

I had taken her cordless phone into the back bedroom of her apartment and closed the door, needing privacy for what I assumed would be a difficult but ultimately productive conversation. She and her boyfriend remained in the living room, but it hardly mattered. The walls were thin, and if things went sideways, they'd hear every word.

I sat there on the edge of her bed as the line rang, hoping for some kind of explanation, some indication that the man I had married still had a shred of decency. Instead, he answered with a dull, emotionless tone, like I was nothing more than a stranger inconveniencing him with my existence.

I must have still believed it was an innocent mistake, that somehow, despite everything, he would follow through on his promise to make sure I could weather the transition as we separated our finances. But when I explained the situation, his response was devoid of any concern.

"Go ask your mother for help," he said flatly, as if it were the most obvious solution in the world.

My mother, a retired widow living on Social Security.

The account was already overdrawn, and I didn't even have money for food, let alone gas to get to work. I sat there, gripping the phone, the crushing reality of his betrayal settling into my chest. He had washed his hands of me completely, and in that moment, I realized just how little I had ever truly known him.

For a solid 30 minutes, I pleaded through uncontrolled, open weeping, my voice cracking under the strain, fighting back gasps for air between sobs. I knew my friends could hear me from the other room, but despite how awkward I knew it must be for them, I couldn't stop. I was drowning and he was the only one who could throw me a lifeline, but he refused.

He didn't just refuse. He seemed to enjoy it.

"Why should I help *you*?" he asked, in a stern tone, my emotion having no effect.

I don't know, Boo Boo. Maybe because it was a joint account? Maybe because you can't just walk out on a lease and pretend the financial consequences don't exist? There were legal obligations, if not moral ones. But none of that mattered to him. I had committed the ultimate sin of being honest about my feelings, and for that I deserved to be punished.

That callousness, that completely detached disregard, was the last thing I ever knew of that man before his divorce papers arrived in the mail without any particular fanfare. There were no more phone calls, no more half-hearted attempts at conversation. Just a clean, final break.

I had no desire to interact with him again, not even digitally.

Kim's friend didn't just have the same first name as my ex, he also was a "junior" just like him. Seeing "Gary Jr." in my email sent a jolt through me, a harrowing moment of shocked disbelief. It was as if a ghost had surfaced from the depths of my past, drudging up old wounds right into my inbox. He hadn't included his last name in the email, so for a few long minutes, I just sat there, staring at the screen.

Once the confusion was cleared up, my new friend changed his email name to avoid any more accidental jump scares. That small gesture of consideration instantly put me at ease, and from there, we started getting to know each other.

At first, our conversations unfolded over email, like a real-life *You've Got Mail* without the deception. Soon after, we moved our conversations into real time on *AIM*. That's *America Online Instant Messenger,* for the folks who have never received a nonstop parade of trial AOL CDs in the mail.

Gary was a divorced father, 10 years older than me, with kids who lived full-time with their mother on the other side of the country.

After his marriage ended, he returned home to Columbia, South Carolina, moving back in with his parents just in time to help care for his father through his sudden illness and eventual passing.

Proudly half Polynesian on his father's side, he'd once had silky dark brown hair, but he kept it shaved to a nub once time began betraying him. His high cheekbones were offset by a well-trimmed dark brown goatee and gray-speckled mustache, which provided a contrast against his light olive skin. He always dressed in bowling shirts and jeans with sneakers, even for work, unless it was summertime, when he would switch to T-shirts and cargo shorts with flip-flops on his days off.

He was intelligent but not particularly cultured, well-spoken but not talkative. He admitted he had never been to see any form of live theatre, but he wasn't a sports fan either. His interests extended exclusively to computers and cars. Otherwise, he was the reserved sort and when he did speak, his voice was hushed and even. Even when he laughed, it sounded restrained, as if the air in his throat was too thick to push an open chuckle through.

And he lived exactly 250 miles away.

Kim knew Gary from their time working together at the regional office of a large consulting firm in Columbia, where she spent her days when she wasn't in Tennessee buzzing around the lake on a jet ski. When Gary was hired into an entry-level desktop support job at the company, Kim was working part-time in the accounts payable section of the accounting department. A friendship emerged as he cleared her work computer of viruses and helped her hide her Leo fan site addiction. Now, two years later, Gary had recently landed a job on the company's network team, but Kim kept him in her back pocket as her personal desktop guru.

The company had a few thousand employees scattered across the globe, supported by an Information Technology staff of over 130 people. Most of the IT Department was based in the Columbia office, managing the majority of user desktop issues remotely. Kim, however, didn't concern herself with logistics. She simply saw a lonely computer geek and decided it was time he established connectivity.

Before we had even met in person, this man was determined. He had a way of making things appear at my door as if by magic. He would ask about my preferences, offer me a selection of gifts to choose from, or just take note of something I mentioned in passing conversation. Almost immediately, whatever it was would show up at my doorstep. Perfume. Surround sound speakers. A designer watch. If I so much as implied a desire, he made sure it materialized at my door within days.

After a month of dazzling me with his willingness to flirt with his credit card limit, he took things a step further. He paid for a DSL line (high-speed internet over landline), freeing me from the agony of watching progress bars inch across the screen while I uploaded my karaoke MP3s.

He also covered the cost of a proper website hosting plan, releasing me at last from the clutches of my GeoCities account and its progressively obnoxious pop-up ads. They were something that had only recently started appearing on free homepages that, until then, had been blissfully clear of anything the webmaster hadn't chosen to put there. Now, they were so obtrusive they made the service almost unusable, signaling the beginning of the end of free home page services and the fan pages that proliferated on them.

Just to ensure we could talk whenever we wanted without the dreaded tally of long-distance charges looming over us, he sent me my very first cell phone. It was a Nokia 3310 with a custom pink shell. The offering felt like the new millennium's version of wearing your high school boyfriend's class ring.

We talked for hours every night, our conversations stretching into the early morning until one of us inevitably drifted off mid-sentence. After all, it wouldn't be a true love story of the early 2000s without the magic words "free nights and weekends." In a time when cell phone use was charged by the minute, it was the best deal available. Those cellular plans ensured that distance was no longer a barrier, and we took full advantage, burning through those unlimited minutes by the hour.

Being spoiled with gifts was a new experience to me and I tried to enjoy it, but I couldn't quite shake the guilt. I barely knew this man, and the last thing I wanted was for either of us to feel any sense of obligation. My efforts to maintain some kind of balance didn't quite work, especially after we met in person. If anything, the gifts only got more extravagant. I couldn't tell if he was overcompensating for something or simply caught up in the euphoria of a new relationship, reckless with his money, showing off, or insecure that he could hold my interest without it. Now, from the 30,000-foot viewpoint, I think I can confidently say it was a little of all of that.

If I had thought the drive between Kingston and Knoxville was too much for a relationship to handle long-term last time, then the 250 miles separating Gary's doorstep from mine proved an even more immediate nuisance. The novelty of long-distance romance wore thin with surprising speed.

For our first in-person meeting, he took an extra day off work and made the drive up to Knoxville for a long weekend. Two weeks later, I returned the favor and drove to Columbia to be his companion while his mother was out of town for a few days. That began our routine of alternating biweekly visits.

Gary's first trip to me was a thoughtfully planned-out weekend designed to familiarize him with the city I had been raised in. It started with a dressed-up date night at a romantic local Italian restaurant, the kind with dim lighting, candlelit tables, and a corner booth with plush curtains that could be closed for privacy. We visited local landmarks, playing tourist at all the most interesting places downtown, and then on the last day of his visit, wound up back at my place with pizza delivery from Harby's Pizza & Deli, my favorite local pizza joint, while we tinkered with my computer and prepared for his return drive home.

That last day of his first visit to Knoxville had been the only time I hadn't scheduled out an activity, which provided the opportunity for it to turn into a test of skill. He sent me into my bedroom for 15 minutes while he stayed in the living room alone. When he finally called me back out, my computer was lying open on the floor, completely gutted with its components scattered around it like a crime scene.

"Now, put it back together," he demanded, motioning toward the electronic carcass. I had spent the last two years learning my way around software, troubleshooting HTML, and pretending to craft custom graphics, but physically rebuilding a computer from scratch? That was a whole different beast. Still, there was no way in hell I was going to let him think I couldn't do it.

At least it was interesting, I'll give him that. I had never been handed a pile of computer parts and told to just go for it before. He didn't guide me, point me in the right direction, or even hint at what to do next. He just sat there, arms folded, waiting to see if I would sink or swim.

That day, I learned that computer parts are just like puzzle pieces. Each one is designed to fit only one way. I hesitated at first, second-guessing myself, but as I started clicking things into place, the logic of it became clearer. The slots, the connectors, the screws. Everything had a purpose and it all made sense once I stopped overthinking it.

I had never even looked inside a computer before. Somehow, I had managed to avoid any real curiosity about how electronics physically worked, focusing instead on what they allowed me to create. As long as they turned on and did what I needed them to do, I never gave much thought to what was happening under the hood. Gary, on the other hand, was all about the guts of the machine. Graphics cards, processors, and motherboards were his playground.

So much so, in fact, that I started calling us "The Hardware Guy and the Software Girl." It was a perfect division of labor. He could rattle off processor speeds, model numbers, and talked about building his own PCs, while I focused on making pretty websites and tinkering with graphics. We spoke the same language, just in different dialects.

My first trip to see him included an underwhelming hour-long driving tour of Columbia where we never got out of the car, lunch at Applebee's, and two days holed up in his mother's house watching movies.

I was officially 0-for-2 in the romance department. First the candlelit dinner I planned for my ex had bombed so badly I never planned anything like it again, and now I was being gifted this long-distance disappointment as reciprocation for my carefully planned, dreamy weekend. I couldn't decide whether to be annoyed or just amused. I convinced myself that it must only be women who put this much thought into planning a date, much less a whole weekend's worth of activities.

I had been searching for someone whose sensibilities more closely matched my own, but I was beginning to give up hope that such a person existed in the South. I felt more metropolitan than my roots suggested. I had always fantasized about being one of those put-together career women striding down New York City sidewalks as if on a mission, sipping wine with dinner while listening to live classical music, and getting invited to chic soirées attended by high-powered Wall Street men in suits.

Instead, all the men around me were blue-collar workers who drove pickup trucks and wore camouflage. When I told them my aunt had paid for me to take violin lessons at the nearby music conservatory as a child, they seemed offended. Some used anti-intellectualism as a security blanket to validate their simpler existence, and my interest in fine arts read like a rejection of it. At least with Gary, for the first time, I felt like I had a partner who genuinely understood and appreciated my tech-driven interests, which, I supposed, would just have to do.

That tag-team pairing worked well when, less than six months into our relationship, I made a decision that stunned everyone. I gave notice at my job and informed my friends and family that I was moving to South Carolina. It wasn't just a leap of faith. It was a catapult into the unknown, powered by equal parts excitement and blind trust.

Leaving Tennessee hadn't even crossed my mind until then. Knoxville was all I'd ever known, but soon, I'd discover I wasn't the only one ready to let go of the past.

One sunny spring afternoon, as I packed and prepared for my upcoming move, I climbed the stairs to my apartment and noticed the door to the unit next to mine standing open. I knew a new neighbor had finally moved in after the apartment had been vacant during my entire three-year stay, but I hadn't realized the full extent of her situation. She had fled an abusive husband, sneaking out in the middle of the night with her children, carrying little more than the clothes on their backs.

As I reached the landing outside our two apartment doors, I caught a glimpse inside. Her kids sat peacefully on a blanket spread across the empty living room floor, transfixed by a small television that rested on a cardboard box. There was no furniture or decorations, just a barren space that spoke volumes about how abruptly she had needed to leave. My sudden departure was her lucky break.

We didn't even need movers. A small U-Haul was enough to hold my personal belongings. Just before we pulled away, I took one last look at my apartment, reminiscing about all those nights sitting in front of my computer screen chatting, then walked to my neighbor's door and left a note.

I let her know I had left my unit unlocked, and that she was welcome to take whatever furniture she needed. It wasn't much, just a mismatched collection of budget pieces and hand-me-downs, but it was enough to make her little family comfortable.

And with that, my life in East Tennessee, the place my family had called home for 10 generations, was over.

Chapter 17: Installing Husband v2.0

Gary was sitting in his underwear on the old sectional his mom had given us when I moved to town. We were still in the trial period, with no guarantees and no paperwork. Our relationship was defined by nothing more than a shared sofa, a shared routine, and a shared cool-down show before bed. In 2003, we were deep into our *Cheers* phase, unwinding each night with the comforting hum of a Boston bar where everybody knew your name, even if, in our world, we were still figuring each other out.

The little house we rented after I moved to Columbia looked like a tiny red brick church from the outside, nestled in a secluded development of nearly identical houses. It was small but perfectly cozy for the two of us, and a welcome relief from the apartment's shared walls and nosy neighbors.

Our daily catch-ups tended to happen on that sofa, in the flickering glow of the television during muted commercial breaks. This was our rhythm, brief pauses in the laughter of *Cheers* to chat about everything from weekend plans and workday frustrations to random childhood memories triggered by the action on the screen. Then, during one such break, he turned to me with the same question he had asked a few times before, the one I had always brushed off with a laugh or by changing the subject.

"Will you marry me?"

There was no bended knee, no elaborate surprise, not even a ring. As much as I had once dreamed of those things, their absence wasn't what had made me turn him down before. Something just felt off. Gary and I were good friends. We seemed to have plenty in common, at least in those early days, but they weren't the things that truly mattered to me and he wasn't good at making me feel like I mattered to him. The lack of effort put toward the proposal hadn't been the first time Gary fell short of even the most basic expectations.

That particular night, an undercurrent of guilt quietly swirled in. Maybe I was being too picky. Maybe I was expecting too much. After all, not only had he showered me with gifts when we first met, but he sold his beloved classic Corvette to get the money to set up house when I moved to town to be with him. It felt like something my father would have done. And so, with the nagging feeling that I was making yet another marital mistake, I said "*yes*."

I had already made plenty of concessions when I moved. Not only had I walked away from the only life and city I had ever known where all of my friends and family were, but I was also learning how to live with someone 10 years my senior. It was someone who, despite still being in his 30s, had all the habits of a retiree.

I was still only 27, still hungry for life after work, restless to be out in the world. When I lived alone, I liked coming straight home after work, then heading back out once traffic died down. I would pop out after dinner to go shopping or driving around, anything to escape the apartment for a little while. I loved taking myself to late movies or out to dinner, and when the mood struck just right, I'd tag along with a friend to a bar. Few things made me happier than sipping a beer at a sidewalk café on a warm summer evening, soft jazz from the live band inside floating on the breeze.

I had always loved the way the night transformed everything, the glow of neon reflected on passing cars, the feeling that those lights had somehow bled their electricity into the atmosphere. But Gary hated going out after dark. He battled through rush hour traffic to run errands on the way home from work, then shut himself in for the night. He behaved as if darkness itself were offensive, something to be locked out like a reverse vampire. Shopping and dining out were strictly reserved for Saturday afternoons.

I learned that lesson the hard way on my 28th birthday, when all I wanted was to dress up and go out to dinner at a nice restaurant. The only problem? The place wasn't open for lunch. That meant he'd have to go out after work, and he made his displeasure about that obvious. He begrudgingly agreed, and I convinced myself he'd come around once we got there. Instead, as we waited for a table, he sat stiffly on a bench out front, irritation oozing from every breath he took. Every attempt at conversation was met with short, clipped replies, like a sulking child.

By the time our food arrived, he still hadn't voluntarily said a word beyond grumbling his order at the server. I couldn't understand how my one simple birthday wish had become such a burden that it ruined his entire day. Even the idea of making someone he supposedly loved happy, just this once, on what was supposed to be my one special day of the year, wasn't enough to make him set aside his discomfort and show me he was glad I had been born.

I stared at the table between us and swallowed hard, fighting back tears. Only later did I recognize the hollow ache that had begun to overtake me, a dawning sense that my needs didn't matter as long as I was "provided for." I hadn't been brought to South Carolina to be loved. I had been brought there to fill a role.

Without warning, I exploded into tears above my chicken parmesan. Across the table, Gary stared at me in stunned horror, paralyzed by the attention the scene had begun to draw. The server stopped by, hesitated for a split second, then turned on his heel and disappeared without a word. Conversations around us hushed, and I could feel the eyes of other diners on me, their glances laced with curiosity, no doubt wondering if they were witnessing a breakup in real time.

Still, he said nothing.

Gary didn't offer comfort and didn't ask what was wrong. He just sat there, staring at me, his only emotion a deep, palpable embarrassment at the public spectacle we had become.

After that incident, I stopped asking him to go out in the evenings and never asked for anything on my birthday again. It wasn't worth the way his response made me feel. The compromise didn't bring me peace. Instead, I just felt trapped. I was in a new city with no family nearby and no real friends outside of a few coworkers I had connected with. To make things worse, we worked in the same office building, which meant everyone I had met in town knew him first.

Is it really so bad? I'd ask myself. At least he was nothing like my first husband, and our coworkers respected him. When he was in the mood to talk, we could have intelligent conversations, the kind that made me feel like we were on the same page. We discussed future goals, like owning that nice little suburban house I had always imagined. When I admitted I wanted to have a child someday so I wouldn't feel like I had missed something in life, he agreed and said he'd be open to it.

All the major plot points aligned.

That hadn't been enough to make me say yes before, but eventually, I suppose I just got tired of him asking.

It's amazing how easy it is to bury apprehensions when there's a party to plan. I had decided I wanted a proper wedding this time, but our budget was impossibly tight. The only venue we could secure was a beach house owned by the entrepreneurial in-laws of my next-to-oldest sister, Robin, in Gulf Shores, Alabama. Normally a vacation rental, it often sat empty in the off-season, so we got the whole place for just the cost of the cleaning fee. We chose January 24, 2004 as the date, since not only did it avoid peak-season rates, it allowed us to have the perfect sunset ceremony without pushing dinner too late into the night.

It would be a destination wedding for both of our families, but the large house helped offset travel expenses by providing overnight accommodations for those who might not have been able to afford the trip otherwise. The house was a duplex disguised as a single, towering four-story beach home, tucked into a row of private oceanfront properties. From the street, you'd never guess it was an income property, split cleanly down the middle into two identical, mirrored units. At the time, we couldn't have afforded even half of it for a weekend, but Robin came through in a pinch and set us up right.

By November 2003, all the plans were in place. I had secured a ball gown-style wedding dress from a secondhand shop for $250, a steal for something that made me feel like a high-end bride without breaking the bank. The cake and flowers were on order courtesy of my mother, and my sister Robin, who ran a catering business in nearby Mobile, had offered to provide the dinner and hors d'oeuvres as a very generous wedding gift.

To save money, I handmade my jewelry and lovingly crafted enough beach-themed favors for each place setting, laboring over every tiny detail for hours to make the day feel like something my first wedding never did… something special.

In true Gen X style, I used Limewire to download four hours' worth of jazz music, clinging to the vain hope that we might get a dance floor going. To improve the odds, I made a list of cheap alcohol to stock up on, figuring liquid courage might do the trick. I drafted Brenda's boyfriend to play DJ for the night and asked Jo Ann to perform *Canon in D* on the keyboard for the wedding procession. Once the rental chairs were reserved, everything was set.

On Thanksgiving Day, just two months before the big day, my mother called me from the hospital. "I was in the middle of making the stuffing, and my chest started to hurt," she said. She had been admitted for the weekend, and open-heart surgery was scheduled for Monday.

I had only been in South Carolina for a year and a half. I didn't have much paid leave saved up at work and knew I needed to hold on to what little I had for the wedding, so we stayed home and monitored the situation from afar. Jo Ann was upset about it. Apparently, it became a hot-button topic, but my mother reassured her that she understood. It never really occurred to me that something would go wrong.

One of the last things she said to me was how upset she was about missing her Thanksgiving dinner. I laughed, trying to keep things light, and told her it would be waiting for her when she got home. But that was a lie.

My phone rang as we pulled into the driveway after work that day. I answered without thinking, expecting another update, but the words hit so starkly I immediately started shaking and dropped the phone. It slid down the inclined driveway toward the gutter, sending me scrambling down the driveway after it.

She never made it out of the surgery. I was an orphan.

After the funeral, we decided to move forward with the wedding, though the joy was gone. It was less like planning a party than a memorial service. I assumed my mother's family would want to rally around us, to make a strong showing in support during our grief, but the guest list dwindled instead. One by one, people dropped out. By the day of the wedding, an invitation list that had started at 150 people had shrunk to fewer than 25.

Maybe it was for the best.

Near the entrance, we set up a memorial table with a photo of Gary's father and planned to do the same with a portrait of my parents, but for all the fuss she made about not coming home for the surgery, Jo Ann forgot to bring it with her from Knoxville. There was no point in getting upset. By then, I had already accepted that the day wasn't going to look the way I had imagined.

My mother's sister was the only one from her side of the family who came. In the end, she stood in for both of my parents, taking my arm and walking me down the aisle, though I hadn't thought to ask her in advance and she had only brought a casual knit outfit to wear.

I will happily give credit where credit is due. Robin knew how to throw a party, even in the midst of a tragedy. On a good day, she could out-Martha Stewart Martha Stewart herself. Her effortless talent always had a way of making me feel like a little girl again, just like when I was 11 years old sitting in the middle school auditorium and bragged to my seatmate, "That's my sister!" when she appeared as Miss Hannigan in the high school production of *Annie*. It always made me feel somehow proud and inadequate at the same time.

The house being a duplex made it perfect for the event. We planned to use the great room on one side for the ceremony and the other for the dinner, which meant we could set up the "dining room" in advance without disrupting anything. Robin provided the table linens and dinnerware, arranged the flowers for the altar, and even crafted an enormous waterfall bouquet of white roses for me.

Brenda had driven in to serve as my Maid of Honor, but the distance had reduced her role to accompanying me to the salon the day of the event before preceding me down the aisle. She had been helping me into my gown in the primary bedroom on the third floor when she stepped out to make sure the coast was clear for my grand entrance. Left alone for the first time all day, I wandered toward the big balcony doors and looked out over the Gulf of Mexico, my beaded dress shimmering in the golden light of sunset. That's when I saw them.

Dolphins, playing in the waves just beyond the surf.

I had never seen wild dolphins before. It felt like they were bringing me their blessing, like a silent moment of grace just for me, a bride on my wedding day.

I had planned a fully formal wedding, but somehow, it still came off low-key. It felt more like a dress rehearsal than the real performance. The sunset ceremony, the catered dinner, and the never-ending flow of cheap champagne and beer couldn't keep the night from ending far earlier than I had expected. My ploy to get what family and friends had shown up onto a dance floor for hours of tipsy, silly fun had failed.

Since we were staying at the beach house, there was no climactic send-off, no lineup of bubble blowers or seed throwers, and no decorated getaway car. There had been nothing to mark the end of the celebration. It sort of just fizzled out, guests slipping away one by one. By 9 p.m., everyone had scattered, leaving me standing in the kitchen of the giant beach house in a formal wedding dress, train and all, with just my new husband, his best friend, and his intoxicated wife.

I've always felt a pang of jealousy watching videos of crowded, hours-long wedding receptions with big dance floors that look more like nightclubs than family affairs. I wondered what it must be like to be the sort of person people naturally flock to. Instead, we were introverts with older families and friends who were married with kids. There was no rowdy after-party, no late-night buffoonery to fill the scrapbooks, just an unremarkable ending to a meticulously planned day. Maybe that's why I was left wondering if it had even been worth all the effort. It had been months of planning for something that never quite lived up to the vision I had in my head.

This time, the whirlpool tub we used for our honeymoon wasn't in a cheap hotel. We had the entire house to ourselves for a few days after the guests cleared out, spending our time listening to the waves roll over the frigid January sand while curled up in front of a fire watching romantic comedies.

The peace, the view, the lingering scent of salt in the air… it felt like the calm after the storm, though I didn't realize then how apropos that would be.

It was my family's last big hurrah in that house. The year before, it had also hosted the wedding of my oldest sister, Ginger, and it was the home Robin and her husband had brought their firstborn back to from the hospital before they bought their permanent home. Although we didn't own it, the house had woven itself into some of our family's biggest milestones, setting the stage for celebrations and new beginnings.

On September 16, 2004, less than a year after our wedding, Hurricane Ivan roared ashore as a Category 3 storm, making landfall directly over the house. It remained standing but only just, battered and broken amid a landscape that lay in ruins.

The lot remains vacant to this day.

If bad omens exist, the dolphins weren't enough to balance this one out.

Chapter 18: If Jump Then Swim

"How the hell do I fix this?" I feverishly typed into AIM, fingers drumming against the keyboard. I bristled at the screen of a computer in the home of a local realtor in Columbia, South Carolina.

This client had found us through the website I built for Columbia Techworks, the freelance computer repair and web design business Gary and I had launched to bring in extra money on the side. I had planned to stick to the "Mr. Hardware-Ms. Software" dynamic and never imagined myself handling in-home repair calls. But when this call came in, my new live-in boyfriend decided it was the perfect opportunity for me to get in a little desktop support experience.

As it turned out, Gary had given me a driver on a USB thumb drive to load onto her computer, and he had saved the wrong version. I had been audibly huffing and sighing in annoyance with myself, believing I was just screwing something up. Though she never let on, I'm pretty sure the client heard me. That was the moment I realized I was not cut out for desktop support.

I left the management track behind in Knoxville before I'd even spent six months as an office manager, and I had decided as a part of my new start in Columbia to try to hitch a ride on the coattails of my network-admin boyfriend into a real Information

Technology career. If I was ever going to make it in IT professionally, though, I knew it would have to be in a role far removed from end-user support. I simply didn't have the temperament for it.

The Columbia Techworks website was one of the few professional-looking sites I ever designed, though in reality, it was mostly a patchwork of simple buttons and scavenged graphics I had modified. I was still in denial that I lacked the skill and training to run a web design business. We only ever landed one paid web design job, and while the paycheck felt significant when it first hit the bank, I quickly realized I couldn't muster the patience required for clients constantly throwing their project behind with last minute tweaks. IT seemed like the easiest path to a legitimate career for someone without a college education, but I needed to find a role that didn't make me want to run for the hills.

I envisioned myself as the introverted IT nerd, isolated in a dark, windowless basement office. The hum of the air conditioning would be the only sound beyond the clicking of my mouse as I silently kept the technological lights on, blissfully removed from the meddling of topside normies who didn't even know I existed. I wanted to be the Goth server room guy from *The IT Crowd.*

As it turns out, that's not what IT actually is. Very few career paths let you work in total isolation. Whether it's end users or other IT folks, people are always part of the equation. Still, I wasn't giving up, I just had to find my niche. For now, it was time to pull the plug on Columbia Techworks. It wasn't providing the easy revenue stream we had imagined.

In the meantime, I was back on the phones, answering the same accounts payable line Kim had been working when she first met Gary. She dropped a recommendation on her supervisor's desk as she left for her early retirement, helping me finally land a job after spending my first two months in town searching for one. The growing stack of bills made being back in a call center-style environment an unplanned but necessary detour in my quest to become an IT professional.

After years of friendship spanning different cities, Kim and I had finally ended up in the same place, yet our paths never quite reconnected. Whether it was just bad timing or an unspoken understanding that our chapter in each other's lives had come to its natural conclusion, I'll never know. After she dropped out of our wedding due to a family emergency, I never saw her again.

If there was anything worse than the appliance call center, I had found it. People calling about money they believed was owed to them were rarely kind. Many were outright hostile. As if that wasn't bad enough, we were also expected to process invoice paperwork between calls. To keep from losing my mind, I turned it into a game, challenging myself to power through as many invoices as possible each day. I was turning out triple the volume of my coworkers, but it wasn't lost on me that I was excelling at a job I absolutely loathed.

Gary assured me that within a year, a vacancy in IT would open up. When it did, we'd spin the Columbia Techworks experience to justify the career change, but everyone knew someone in Columbia's IT circles. They tended to travel in packs like wolves, following their favorite manager to the next big opportunity, leaving their old company with a set of vacancies for the next pack to fill. Breaking in from the outside was damn near impossible.

I knew someone, sure enough. Gary was becoming the right-hand man of the IT Infrastructure Manager, who would've done just about any favor he asked for. Would that be enough to make my "experience" outshine the guy someone else knew? Human Resources still had the final say, and even in that small city, connections could only get you so far.

A year passed. Then two. Then two more. When a position opened on the same team as the enterprise webmaster, I put in an application without even reading the job description. I didn't care whether it was a junior webmaster position or a content editor role, I just wanted to get my foot in the door.

When I interviewed with the hiring manager, Randy, he was not impressed with having me shoehorned onto his team by the infrastructure manager. "This job will be a *very* steep learning curve for you," he warned, but I wasn't going to let him deter me. All I needed was a chance to prove myself.

It took a full year just to get my application off the finance manager's desk, even with the infrastructure manager's endorsement. Getting it through HR with my lack of experience was an even tougher game of back and forth. Documenting something that barely existed felt like squeezing the last drop of toothpaste out of the bottom of the tube, but somehow, we managed it.

Leaving accounts payable wasn't as easy as I'd expected. I knew the work inside and out. It was familiar. Comfortable. Reliable, even. On my last day, the anxiety ran so high I had tunnel vision. Everything passed in a blur of well-wishers stopping by to say goodbye, even though I was only moving to a private office directly above the one I'd occupied for six years, just four floors up.

Four floors up. That was it. So why did it feel like I was drifting away like an untethered balloon, completely unsure of where I'd land? The only thing I knew is that I had *a* job, but no one had explained what it was going to be.

And so began my professional IT career, with an internal OH GOD, HERE WE GO as if I were perched at the peak of a roller coaster, bracing for the plunge. I was now the newest Systems

Administrator for an international consulting company, part of the Windows server team.

Servers. Wait… what?

I had found myself in an IT department of around 130 employees that supported everything from user desktop computers to application development. It turned out that Heather, the senior webmaster, only occupied the office next to my new one and wasn't actually on my team. Instead, I found myself working on a team of men with a wide variety of server related specialties.

Heather was an earthy, progressive woman in her mid-30s who was just tall and gangly enough to be slightly accident prone. I was constantly hearing her knock things over through the thin wall that separated our small offices. She had a childlike honesty and kind spirit that was easy to befriend, especially in a sea of men. Even though she wasn't on my team, there were many days when she was the only one who understood what I was going through.

I had been told to expect to feel like I was drowning for a good six months before I'd finally get my legs beneath me. My six-month mark had arrived in early 2010, and I was still flailing, gasping for air in a sea of unfamiliar responsibilities.

My team was divided into two sections that covered three layers of support. In Operations, the least experienced first-tier staff handled daily support requests from the ticketing queue, while second-tier staff took on advanced troubleshooting and project work. The coveted third-tier roles made up the Systems Engineering team, making decisions about the environment and drafting policies. As the newest junior systems administrator in Operations, my role was entry-level server support, but it was far from entry-level IT.

Even newcomers to Operations with years of desktop support under their belts faced an uphill climb if they had Engineering ambitions. The constant stream of operational tasks left little time for on-the-job training. In my case, *no one* was excited to train the "new girl" (emphasis on *girl)* with no professional IT experience *at all.* I was quickly discovering what Randy meant by "a steep learning curve."

I began to have panic attacks any time a ticket landed in my queue that I didn't know how to handle. Needing to escalate a ticket to second-tier support felt like a failure, a booming announcement that I was in over my head. More than anything, I couldn't stand the idea of embarrassing my husband. I wanted so badly to prove that those who had fought to put me in this job had been right, that I wasn't just some charity case or mistake. I needed to prove that I had earned my place here. I didn't want to be pushed into a corner and thought of as dead weight.

Less than a year after I transferred into IT, a second-tier position opened and I was promoted, but mostly only because I was the last remaining tech in a lower job title. When he backfilled my original job afterward, Randy brought in someone with much more experience than I had and assigned him the second-tier work I had been hoping for. I had a higher title, but he had the better role.

Before the new hire was chosen, Randy promised that I would get the next available spot in Systems Engineering as a reward for what he called "a dogged determination" to learn. He must've thought that day was years away. I had the drive, but I was still very shaky, something Randy noted when he pointed out that I needed to work on my confidence. I don't think I was *surprised* when the new guy also got the Engineering job a year later. I was just disappointed in *myself.*

"It's okay to be angry. You *should* be," Randy said when he broke the news. The new guy even apologized for getting my promotion. They had all expected me to blow a fuse, but instead, I just nodded. He wasn't wrong to choose the more seasoned tech, but being stuck watching the first-tier work queue wasn't giving me the broader troubleshooting experience I needed. I was locked in a catch-22.

The only good thing about being stuck in *Groundhog Day* hell was that I was getting damn good at that first-tier role. The daily support requests were the job's bread and butter, but I had accidentally landed in a position that felt uncomfortably close to a customer service call center job. Any time someone had their name regularly appear as the assigned technician on those tickets, end users who were frightened of technology would latch onto them, bypassing protocols to pester them relentlessly anytime something didn't quite work as they expected. That's why *no one* wanted to be associated with the ticket queues.

I spent hours creating step-by-step instructions that required no technical background to follow, convinced it would help deter repeat offenders. Honestly, I think I missed my calling as a technical writer. I've always enjoyed crafting beautifully structured documents with clearly labeled screenshots, as if I were writing a "Computers for Beginners" workbook.

The trouble was, the more I tried to hand them the tools that would help them help themselves, the less interested they seemed. They didn't want cheat sheets and how-to guides. They didn't want to learn so they wouldn't have to ask for help. They just wanted someone else to do it, and often acted offended as if I were refusing to do my job when I offered the instructions instead.

It was just like the appliance call center all over again. This was *worse* than dealing with end users in desktop support. This was dealing with people who just didn't want to learn how the software on their own computer worked.

At least I was having fun while I was at it. I loved teasing the male techs about their "nice rack" as they worked on a server mounted in one of those black, cage-like shelving units, watching the flicker of amusement cross their faces when they realized they couldn't return the compliment without risking an HR violation. My favorite dad joke, however, was texting Gary from the server room, a meat locker kept at 65 degrees so the heat from hundreds of servers wouldn't warp the equipment. After half an hour in there rebuilding a server one afternoon, I typed: "I'm freezing off my ba... OH MY GOD, THEY'RE GONE!"

Heather's friendship became especially crucial to my mental health when the men on my team seemed to close ranks, keeping me at arm's length from the infrastructure I was so determined to learn. More often than not, she would reach out to comfort me before I even recognized something had bothered me. In return, I became her soft place to land whenever Sheila, the content editor on her team, started in on her.

Sheila was a woman in her mid-50s with thin, dyed-red hair that she kept carefully styled into a short hairspray helmet. She spoke in a high-pitched, childish tone that reminded me of baby Miss Piggy from the nursery scene in *The Muppets Take Manhattan*. She was a voracious gossip, known for her cattiness, and the one thing she didn't appreciate was Heather's cross-team alliance with me. Her desk was tucked around the corner in an open area that had been meant for a receptionist, so Heather and I were grateful to have offices where we could enjoy venting to each other behind closed doors.

What we weren't prepared for was how vital that arrangement would become to our survival over the coming two years. A major shakeup was just beyond the horizon, one that would dethrone Sheila as the IT department's reigning villain and introduce a whole new set of challenges.

Chapter 19: Binary Battle Royale

In the spring of 2012, a new technology director named Tilly was hired and all of management above Randy cycled out. Tilly was best described as a "Walmart Miranda Priestly," striding through the hallways shouting orders and dressing down managers in meetings as though fear were the same thing as respect. She wasn't fooling anyone. Her devil's Prada was really bargain-bin couture.

Tilly was purportedly brought in to streamline IT and immediately set to work on a departmental reorganization. She kept a copy of the organizational chart on her desk, covered in Post-it notes, each one marking some secret change in the works. Her paranoia ran so deep that she locked her office door every time she stepped out, even just to use the bathroom, as if someone might sneak in and uncover her diabolical plan while she was sitting on the toilet playing Angry Birds. She was intentionally cultivating an environment of suspicion and fear.

A few months in, I was pulled aside and told that Tilly was considering transferring my position, along with me in it, to the web team. She had reviewed the work history on my application and decided that it would be a better bang for the company's buck. Perhaps she thought she was doing me a favor. Two years earlier, I might've agreed. I had learned to code BASIC and HTML on my own, and if I put in the effort, I knew I could learn CSS and JavaScript, too.

But for the past two years, I had been breaking my back to learn how to support server infrastructure. If I were reassigned, everything I had worked for, everything I had fought through debilitating anxiety to achieve, would be wiped away in an instant.

With only two years of experience in my first-tier role, finding another IT infrastructure job wouldn't be easy. Most employers expected a foundation in desktop support, something I had ironically insisted I didn't want. I began submitting applications to every job I could possibly qualify for, but had not received a single callback.

Randy and I began searching for any ammunition he could use to argue for keeping me where I was. I enrolled in training classes and began earning certifications, ones that were only relevant to infrastructure work, nothing that would support a transition to the web team. We knew it was a long shot, but it was the only proactive thing I could do.

Luckily, I still had my ally, Heather. She had regular closed-door conferences with the web team manager about how transferring me to their team wouldn't make sense. Everyone in management seemed to agree, it wasn't a good idea. Everyone except Tilly who *raged* when anyone pushed back against it.

Sheila was already positioning herself to claim seniority over me the moment the transfer became official, despite the fact that, in title, we would be equals. She spent hours smugly complaining from inside the web manager's office down the hall, purposefully loud enough for everyone to hear, every time I failed to jump the moment her support requests landed in my queue.

It was a game Heather and I both knew well. She'd tried angling to unseat Heather through the same passive-aggressive maneuvering not long before. Sheila never seemed to want Heather's job, only to dominate her, as though Heather merely having the title "Senior Webmaster" somehow bruised her ego.

Between Sheila and Tilly, the following two years were abject misery. I kept my head down and ground through the daily work, week after week, hoping to catch even a hint of a light at the end of the tunnel. Then, one day, a spotlight broke through the gloom.

In November 2013, we received word that the Board of Directors had become disenchanted with Tilly's lack of results and fired her without warning. They finally recognized what we had all seen firsthand: you can't streamline anything with a wrecking ball. One day she was there lording over us, and the next she was gone. She never even got to have a farewell cake in the break room.

She hadn't even finished implementing most of her reorg, but the damage had already been done. We had lost a significant amount of talent, including most of management between her and Randy. What remained was a gutted team, stretched thin, trying to salvage the remnants of a directionless vision that had never truly made sense.

Randy happened to catch a glimpse of her in the moments after she'd been relieved of duty. Tilly dropped heavily into the chair outside her office door, like the wind had just been knocked out of her, staring into the distance as she processed the shock. I might've felt sympathy if she hadn't spent the past two years terrorizing everyone beneath her on the org chart. As it stood, it was a well-earned comeuppance.

As Thanksgiving approached, I stood in a half-empty data center with what was left of our server team, huddled around a virtual host like a team of doctors debating a treatment plan. Across the room, server racks stripped bare by a recent virtualization project sat shoved into a corner, waiting to be hauled off like old furniture. I stared at them and pretended to listen while my coworkers prattled on about redundant power cabling.

Randy appeared at the end of the aisle as if from thin air. He caught my eye and motioned for me to come to him. "Come with me," he called over the roaring white noise of the machines, his voice just piercing enough to cut through it.

Without another word, he turned and walked out, leading me away from the others. He marched through the heavy data center doors and straight to the elevator with determined purpose. After the doors slid shut, he took a deep breath and turned toward me. "Just act like you're happy to have the opportunity," Randy said with ominous undertones, pressing the button for the floor where Tilly's now-vacant office sat in darkness.

Seated at a small, round meeting table in the corner of Tilly's old office were two people already waiting for us. One was the web manager. The other was the finance manager, Barbara, the woman whose bureaucratic roadblocks had nearly derailed my entire career before it even started.

She wasted no time. With her usual coldness, Barbara handed us copies of a revised position description form with my name at the top and, in her most matter-of-fact tone, explained that I was being reassigned to the web team. Tyranny Tilly was gone. Her grand vision for restructuring had been cut short.

And yet, they were doing it anyway.

After both managers made their arguments for why it wasn't a good idea, Barbara sat back in her seat as a scowl formed on her face. "The ship has sailed," she said arrogantly, as though she had the authority of a CIO. It was all very callous. To her, my entire career path was just a formality to be shuffled around on a finance spreadsheet without my consent.

In the end, the two managers came to a reluctant agreement. I would keep doing exactly what I had been doing all along, only now, the web manager would be the one signing my timesheets until they could figure out a better solution.

We had all celebrated Tilly's departure, but that meeting was like discovering a crack in the foundation the day after closing on a new house. Before Christmas, Randy resigned for a job he'd applied to back when he thought Tilly was there for the long haul, taking several team members with him to his new company. I was so busy keeping my head above water that I hadn't noticed what it meant. Once everyone else left, *I* was a senior tech.

There was no promotion or recognition, only the new reality that dozens of systems had no one but me to support them. More critically, I was the only person in the company with access to the virtual infrastructure which had nearly 500 servers running on it.

The higher-level techs had been sent to expensive week-long training courses before they quit, but now there wasn't even any management left to approve training for me. I spent what little downtime I had putting myself through my own crash-course, building and abusing virtual machines to learn the ins and outs of the platform before something failed.

How had I gone from wobbling like a newborn foal to holding the reins of an international company's entire virtual infrastructure in under four years, all from a junior position in Operations?

A new technology director was brought in by March 2014, along with an entirely new management team to replace those that Tyranny Tilly had run off. All at once, I had a bright, high-energy infrastructure manager and his right-hand man as my supervisor, both trusted former employees of the new director from their last company.

While they immediately reversed the decision to reassign me to the web team, they hadn't replaced any of the technicians who left. The entire Engineering team was dismantled. As my consolation prize, they traded my lower-tier position for a much-overdue mid-tier promotion, but I was still in Operations and would never be able to achieve the Engineering position I had been aiming for. It simply didn't exist anymore.

My new supervisor, whom the new director described as a "rock star," assumed all the third-tier work himself while the rest of us were permanently relegated to the daily operational tasks. *Time for me to go row with the other slaves.*

We had all been siloed into our own support areas, with no backup beyond the supervisor, who was perpetually overwhelmed. I was still managing the work queues, and now I was also taking on whatever operational work in the virtual environment my supervisor didn't have time to do. I was operating at full tilt with no relief on the horizon, and, worse, no one seemed to notice. That is, until one sunny spring afternoon when I broke down in tears right there in the office.

That was also the day I learned Sheila had taken credit for the entire library of documentation I had created, all the old instructions I had updated, all the processes I had worked tirelessly to format into easy-to-follow guides. She must've been frustrated that the groundwork she had laid in preparation for my joining her team had been in vain, and she seemed to take any opportunity to undermine me as my penalty for escaping reassignment.

That afternoon, overwhelmed and exhausted, I finally snapped.

I sat in my office, stifling my sniffles, hot tears of resentment spilling down my face. When I finally got up and rushed outside to go home, Sheila followed, her voice laced with sappy, performative sympathy as she asked what had happened to cause my distress. I wasn't certain she knew she was the reason I had broken, though it would have undoubtedly pleased her.

For years, Sheila had been loudly taking jabs at me behind my back, timing them for when the hallway was quiet to ensure I would overhear the performances she put on in the web manager's office. If she had done it to my face, I wouldn't have known how to react and would've given her the satisfaction she craved. But, as with most bullies, she was a coward who seemed to be daring me to confront *her* instead. That was the one thing I knew I would *never* give her.

Stealing credit for my work was a low blow, even for Sheila. Feigning support so she could get the gossip on why I was upset only poured salt on the wound. As I rushed out to my car, wiping tears and blowing snot bubbles the whole way, Sheila was right on my heels, trying to pry it out of me. I just shooed her away and drove off, catching a glimpse of her standing there looking perturbed in my rearview mirror as I sped out of the parking lot.

The worst part was this wasn't her first rodeo. She had done the same thing to Heather a year earlier. We had all watched Heather spin out into an anxiety purgatory during a high-profile site redesign project. It was so grueling that it left her with stress-induced hair loss, thinning her once-thick mane of long, chestnut-brown hair to a scrawny rope of a ponytail.

I remembered seeing them collaborating and getting annoyed at Heather when she insisted Sheila hadn't done everything she was trying to take credit for. I may have known Sheila to be a bully, but I couldn't believe anyone would do the brazen things Heather claimed she was doing. What I didn't know was that when I saw them together, Sheila was usually just venting about her personal drama while Heather busily combed through lines of HTML and CSS code.

Sheila would join Heather at a nearby diner after work, supposedly to help her sort through pages of outdated code. In reality, she might've helped her hunt for a stray tag once in a while, but almost all of the work fell to Heather. Sheila's rare contributions came only when it suited her, and the rest of the time was spent crafting the illusion that she was more involved than she really was. As much as I wanted to take her side, from the outside looking in, it fully looked like Heather was just ungrateful for Sheila's help.

When the time came to hand out accolades for the redesign project, Sheila was the first one in line ready to accept her pat on the back. She didn't just accept the praise, she *demanded* credit for the work just for being in the room while Heather did it. Even when Heather confronted her about exaggerating her involvement, Sheila arrogantly insisted, "We'll just have to agree to disagree about that."

I believed Heather now. Sheila was doing the same thing to me.

I stopped pretending to tolerate Sheila and became as cold toward her as professionally possible. It would be a long time before I could even say her name without recoiling. Within another year, she left the company in a huff, furious that she hadn't been offered the senior webmaster job when Heather, finally at her limit, vacated it. Neither of us realized until later that management had seen right through Sheila's charade and never intended to elevate her beyond the level of content editor.

Over the next several years, all I could feel was my wheels spinning. Allowing a supervisor to take on all the third-tier work alone had set us up for failure once he left. The vacant Engineering positions that were traded away to other teams when he took over their work were never returned.

I tried to train new staff on the first-tier support tasks whenever we hired someone into the junior position, but either they weren't a good fit or recognized it as the undesirable grunt work that it was and left in short order. Some couldn't make it past the initial six-month break-in period when even experienced techs were in a constant state of confusion. I suppose they could have been fleeing my negativity, too. I was growing increasingly disgruntled at my own lack of progress and wasn't bothering to hide it.

When a contractor was brought in to take over the virtualization work, the one thing I had left that kept me grounded to Engineering-level work was gone too. I was desperate to integrate myself into new areas of support, but one thing kept dragging me back like the antagonist in a horror movie, grabbing my ankle just when I thought I'd gotten away.

What was left of my soul died when the latest infrastructure manager introduced me as the "Ticket Lady" to a new supervisor he'd just hired for another section.

It had been over 10 years since I left accounts payable. For well over half that time I'd been training new hires and handling second-tier work, so it never even crossed my mind that this was how he saw me. Not even my own manager could recognize me as anything more than the woman who managed the first-tier queues.

I was getting a reputation for being difficult and angry. And what's worse, *I no longer cared.* By the end of 2019, I had begun looking for other work.

Chapter 20: Failure to Authenticate

"Why were you talking to him about *that*?"

The question was unconcerned in tone, but Gary's eyes weren't.

It had to have been around 2008 when I began to feel the first breezes of the coming storm front, barely four years into the marriage. I already knew Gary had a jealous streak. He made that clear while we were still just dating.

At first, it was just teasing. Anytime I chatted with one of the few men on my accounts payable team, he'd taunt: "There goes your boooyfriiiend," stretching out the word in a sing-song taunt as my coworker walked by. It was annoying, but I ignored it, chalking it up to innocent playfulness. But when I got the job on the server team, a group made up entirely of men, the teasing transitioned into something else.

Suddenly, wanting to be friends with my coworkers wasn't just an excuse for his loaded comments, it was a full-blown issue. "Why can't you find a woman to talk to?" he'd ask, as if I were choosing my coworkers like picking a seat in a high school cafeteria. If he walked into our team's hallway to collect me for lunch and saw me socializing in a male coworker's office, I would get the silent treatment.

Eventually, one drunken night, Gary blurted out the truth. It wasn't other men he didn't trust around me. It was me he didn't trust around them. It was an entirely unfounded accusation. I had never cheated on anyone and never intended to.

I should've left then, but ever determined not to learn from my mistakes, I ignored the break points and trudged forward. I was convinced it was more important to honor my commitment than to acknowledge my emotional needs. The disastrous birthday dinner that first year after I moved should have made it clear they didn't matter in this relationship anyway, but I hadn't recognized it yet.

We were both working full-time and eventually I would even be making more money than him, but he wanted to be seen as the provider, to make sure I had clothing, shelter, and food. Just not much else. Anytime I needed something that wasn't a "fun" purchase, he would grumble about the expense. He reacted to a dentist bill like I'd gone out and spent the grocery money on a new designer bag. He was better at making me feel like a burden than making me feel loved, but then, I had grown up understanding that dynamic all too well.

As the youngest child in a blue-collar family, I was often told we couldn't afford the things I asked for, like so many other kids. With four kids to drain the family coffers, making any sort of request was usually met with frustration. While other kids talk about their parents making sure they never felt the burden of their financial situation, we were acutely aware of it at all times.

School clothes shopping meant one pair of jeans and five shirts, despite the bullying that would invariably result in. In the '80s, it wasn't just about not having a different outfit every day. Being a preteen without the money to participate in all those over-the-top trends was downright painful.

Speaking of painful, we only saw a dentist or doctor if we had an ailment that would worsen without treatment. I was one of those kids who always seemed to have an ear infection, so that approach eventually led to permanent hearing loss in one ear. By 22, I had also already had my first root canal and discovered I had always needed glasses, after never having been taken to the dentist or optometrist until I could pay for it myself.

I'd been conditioned to believe that any amount spent on my needs was too much, so when Gary started treating me the same way, it was expected behavior. I should've pushed back, but instead I accepted it as his way of saying, "you're not worth this," a subtle confirmation of something I already feared. Now, he was becoming controlling on top of it.

I was suffocating, caught in the tightening grip of Gary's insecurities. When he was referred for a job at another company across town, I encouraged him to take it, pitching it as a smart career move. In truth, it was an act of quiet self-preservation, a way to relieve some of the pressure that had been building between us. I couldn't stand being around him 24/7 anymore. He saw through the scheme, admitting later that he hadn't wanted to take the job but felt I had pressured him, either unwilling or uninterested in confronting what was really happening between us.

All it took was a little breathing room before I slipped back into my old habit of fantasizing that he didn't exist. The days of unwinding together with cool-down shows before bed were long gone, replaced by an unspoken agreement to live parallel lives. He would slip away to bed while I stayed at my computer, my online activities stretching out the hours until I finally wandered off to bed by myself, usually in a different room.

At some point, I stopped waiting for him to engage. I was tired of his emotional absence, tired of always being the one to try. If he wasn't going to fully show up, then I didn't want him there at all.

The distance between us only widened as the trouble at work escalated under the reign of Tyranny Tilly. He never understood what my job entailed, let alone why I was so distraught over the possibility of losing it. Anytime I tried to talk to him about my day, he would just stare, his body language carrying the same message every time: *Why are you even talking?*

By September of 2014, I'd had enough. One evening, I simply announced that I was moving out. Gary didn't argue, didn't ask why, and didn't try to stop me. I found out later that he had already discussed the possibility with his best friend. It had come as no surprise. So without a word, he turned, walked into the bedroom, and closed the door behind him.

The chasm between us had grown so wide there could be no denying it any longer. After years of walking on eggshells whether I was conscious of it or not, leaving was the only move I had left. I could support myself now, even if it meant accepting my fate as the Operations Queen. But one thing was certain… something had to change.

Early in our relationship, he had played a risky game of bait-and-switch, but now that same deception was working in my favor, paving the way for my escape. Before we were married, he had assured me he was open to having another child since I hadn't had any yet. I was never certain I wanted one but I didn't want to rule it out, either. The ink was barely dry on the marriage license when I discovered he had tricked me.

The last time I saw Kim at her lake house, the summer before I moved to South Carolina, wasn't the last time I went there. Gary and I returned a few months after our wedding for a "second honeymoon," a serene weekend meant for grilling out beneath the screened-in porch and waving to passing boats from the dock. That first evening, after lighting a fire and popping open a bottle of Cold Duck in Kim's honor, we also lit a fuse.

I don't remember what prompted it. Maybe I'd been musing about how long it might take before I'd want to start trying to get pregnant.

"I've already had my kids," he said, his tone cold and unyielding.

The next morning, I sat alone on the dock, wrapped in a blanket, watching the morning fog hug the glassy surface as the sun rose over the still, silent water. I had spent hours grappling with what had transpired the night before. I remember feeling disappointed, but I hadn't let myself acknowledge it as betrayal. Not yet.

I don't know how our young marriage survived that moment, except that by then, I already felt trapped. I was living hundreds of miles away from the friends who had been my lifeline the first time I needed to run. He managed our finances, and between us, there was never much left over, certainly not enough for me to break free with.

But now, 10 years later, things were different. I was established. I didn't need support. And without kids to anchor me to him, I could leave whenever I needed to. So I did.

I moved into a two-story townhouse five miles from the home we had bought together right after the wedding. It was rented with a small stash of cash I'd squirreled away over three years, $20 at a time, so he wouldn't notice it missing. I'd always feared a final, explosive argument that would force a quick escape. I knew I would need cash if that day came to avoid the same situation that happened with the first Gary Jr. The fund barely covered the cost of a sofa, yet the fact that I had it at all convinced me I was making the right move.

A sofa was just the beginning. I had an entire house to fill, and for the first time in a long time, I was doing it for myself. It was overwhelming, but in the best possible way, a burden that felt more like freedom.

I've learned to see these moments less as endings and more like opportunities to start over. A bright, clean house. New things. New surroundings. It's not quite reinvention, but it carries that same nervous excitement as the first day of school. Everything feels open, full of possibilities, like stepping into a new homeroom in brand-new clothes, full of the radiant hope that maybe, just maybe, this time things will be different.

That feeling only lasted a few days before the first landmine he had planted went off, shaking the foundation of my carefully built escape.

A frantic call came in one morning just as I was leaving for work. It was Randy, my former supervisor, someone I hadn't heard from in years. I had long since become suspicious of his role in the mess Tyranny Tilly left behind. Time had given me the clarity of thought I needed to take inventory of the things he could've done to prevent my career stalling out in Operations. I wasn't still angry about it, but I'll admit there was still a little salt left under the edges. Hearing his voice again was an unexpected reminder of a moment in time I'd much rather forget.

"They called me because they thought I would have your number," he said. "He's been taken to the hospital."

Had Gary really not told his coworkers we were no longer together? I supposed not. Maybe it was pride, or maybe he didn't want to admit it to himself. Either way, it didn't matter now. I was already on my way to the hospital to sit by the side of a man who wouldn't even allow his doctor to tell me what was wrong.

But I didn't need an explanation. I knew. My leaving had made him unravel, and his body had finally begun to reject the self-medicating he had turned to in response. His way of coping had always been predictable. The only question now was how bad it had gotten, but I couldn't let him pull me back in. I couldn't let his downward spiral become my own. If I wavered, if I let guilt worm its way in, I risked undoing everything I had fought so vigorously to establish. I had to step back and defend that boundary with everything I had. The rest of my life depended on it.

When he checked himself out of the hospital against his doctor's advice, there was nothing I could do to stop him. He was determined to handle things his way, even if that meant not handling them at all. I told him I would keep him on my insurance until he got treatment, hoping he would take the offer. He refused.

The medication the hospital had given Gary, in combination with his inability to stop self-medicating, kept him nearly comatose. He never left the house and barely got out of bed. His boss started calling daily, first begging him for medical documentation to explain his absence and then begging me to find a way to obtain it on his behalf before he was forced to fire him But what could the doctor provide? If he refused treatment, he refused the medical excuse that came with it. Within a month, he had lost his wife and his job. The house would be next. Still, he did nothing.

With time running out, I warned that I would have him placed on an involuntary hold if he didn't get help. His response was chilling. He threatened to shoot himself if anyone he didn't know showed up at the house or if he so much as spotted an ambulance outside. Soon after, he started sleeping with a loaded gun in the bed beside him, neutering me of any options I may have had to help.

Above all, I was angry. After everything I had already endured, this was the final insult. I couldn't stop myself from thinking this was some twisted attempt at manipulation, a last-ditch effort to force me into staying. I wasn't going to let it work. I *couldn't* let it work.

I called his brother in to monitor him, to find some way to help him. The only thing I knew for certain was *I* couldn't be the one to do it.

Unable to pay the mortgage, Gary abandoned the house we once shared to move in with his mother who had retired several years before. He walked away as if it were nothing, leaving behind most of his possessions, requiring me to swoop in, handle the mess myself, and get it rented before it slipped into default. Not because I cared what happened to it, but because I had no choice. My name was on the mortgage, and if I didn't take immediate action, it would tank my credit, another consequence of his recklessness that I refused to shoulder.

The new tenants had barely settled in when I found out he had grown tired of his mother's strict rules and had gone to stay with his brother. He brought Gary by one afternoon to pick up a box of belongings, and for the first time in months, we stood face to face. Gary told me he had found another job and was getting back on his feet. I nodded, kept things civil, and left it at that. Despite everything, I didn't want to add to his stress by pressuring him to finalize the divorce while he was still recovering.

After that, I'm not sure what happened. A few months passed with nothing but silence between us. Finally, after deciding it was time to tie up some loose ends, I changed my email address and sent out a mass update, BCC'ing all my important contacts, including him.

His daughter responded from his account.

"Dad's in hospice care. You should probably come see him soon."

I had no idea things had gotten that far. I had imagined that he was working his new job, settling into a little apartment somewhere, piecing together a new life. That was the version I had held onto, the one I had chosen to believe. After all, he hadn't told me any different. No one had.

Instead, reality had taken a much darker turn. Without my knowledge, his health had continued to decline until his brother could no longer care for him, forcing him to move in with his adult daughter, who had only just moved back to town as it was all starting to unravel. He hadn't even seen her since she was a small child, and now they were out of time.

I reread her email, turning the words over in my mind, trying to make sense of them.

But no. No, I couldn't go see him.

I was too angry. Too angry at him, too angry at his family, too angry at the way it seemed he had orchestrated it all so that I would always carry the crushing guilt for leaving, no matter how impossible it had been to stay. I knew that if I went to see him, it would only be another negative memory. There was nothing left to say, nothing that could undo the years of resentment. Going to see him would only open the door for an even worse final impression that I would always regret.

And yet, not knowing exactly what was happening made the guilt worse. I had handed the ball off to his family, trusting that they would get him the help he needed while I focused on salvaging what was left of my own life. But had they dropped the ball? Worse, had they enabled his downfall? Should I have come back and tried to stop it, even knowing it would have cost me everything? These are unanswered questions that will plague me for the rest of my life.

Then, in October 2015, I got a call at work from an unknown number. It went to voicemail. The message was brief, almost casual. It was from Gary's cousin, calmly asking me to return his call.

How odd. His family never called me, much less his cousin, whom I'd only met a handful of times. A familiar sense of dread washed over me. On impulse, I searched his name.

And that's when I found it. His obituary.

Staring at the screen, I braced myself for a wave of emotion that never came. I was shocked not by what I felt, but by what I didn't. I felt nothing.

When I finally returned the call, I learned the only reason I had been contacted at all. We hadn't yet filed for divorce. As his surviving spouse, I was required to sign off on his cremation.

It was over. I was an orphan and a widow, all before the age of 45.

Chapter 21: Clearing the Cache

Moving back into my house felt less like returning to the scene of the crime and more like wiping the slate clean. The townhouse had been a comfortable placeholder, but the knowledge that it was temporary kept me from truly settling in. *This* house was mine, and I had the deed to prove it. Before he moved out, I had Gary sign it over to me, lock, stock, and barrel. Now, it was my refuge, my new start. At long last, I wasn't running from something. I was moving toward something better.

The tenants had moved out just before my own lease expired in the spring of 2016, and I wasted no time getting to work. Every evening and weekend, I was there, brush in hand, reclaiming the space one paint stroke at a time. I painted the walls a lighter, warmer taupe, except for a few brightly colored accent walls that made me irrationally happy. I hung new window treatments to let light flood in, chasing away the heavy oppression that had lingered like a stain for so many years.

I replaced the windows and doors, had the roof redone and new flooring installed, and even rebuilt the backyard fence. Each upgrade seemed to peel away another layer of the past. I rearranged the furniture until the space no longer resembled the same prison I had once been trapped in. Instead, it became a sanctuary, a place where I could heal, not just exist. I felt happy for my little house, almost as if it were healing with me. I even started calling it my "little cottage," to help solidify its new identity. It was the same structure I had lived in for more than a decade, but for the first time, it began to feel like my home.

The house was still small, still flawed in ways that occasionally annoyed me, but over time, I grew to love spending most of my time there. The last time I lived alone, I constantly felt the call of the road, the need to escape the confines of my little apartment for an hour or two, even if I had nowhere to go. But not here. Here, I could cocoon myself away from the world, in the safety of the home I had made for myself.

Every weekend I took myself shopping for new décor pieces, with one rule: I wouldn't buy anything unless it practically called my name. Over time, the house filled with knickknacks, vases, and wall hangings that warmed my soul every time I looked at them. Maybe I had once thought spending money on those things was frivolous, or maybe that was just what I told myself when I thought we couldn't afford them. Either way, I understood their value now.

As I moved back in, I'd filled the single-car garage nearly to the ceiling with boxes, and for weeks it looked less like a place to park a car than the set of an episode of *Hoarders: The Moving Edition.* Bit by bit I chipped away at the stacks, until finally only one box was left, wedged against the back wall between the washer and dryer.

It was an old Xerox paper box I'd been dragging from house to house since leaving Knoxville, held together by brittle tape that had yellowed at the edges. Inside was a time capsule that smelled faintly of dust and 1999: a mountain of glossy magazines, each one crowned with the same face on the cover, as familiar to me as old family photos.

I couldn't help myself. I sat cross-legged on the concrete floor, flipping through the stack, stopping to admire my old favorite spreads. Some of the fragrance ads still puffed out their stubborn perfume, as if daring me to remember the boy-band era of Tommy Girl and CK One. And then there he was again: that floppy curtain haircut falling over one eye, that sly, world-conquering grin. Instantly, I wished to be 23 again, discovering Leo for the first time and letting myself fall hopelessly in love with the caricature I had created, a blend of Romeo's passion and Jack Dawson's scrappy perceptiveness.

At the very bottom, tucked flat against the cardboard, I found something I hadn't seen in years. I'd already filled most of the wall space in the house, but for this, I'd make room. I carried it inside, hammered a tack into the wall by my bedroom window, and straightened the wooden frame until it sat perfectly aligned.

"Hello, old friend," I said, brushing away the dust from the glass over the autograph. I guess I'll never really know if it was real, but it never mattered. The idea of it was real enough.

I made plans to stay until retirement and mapped out what the rest of my life there might look like. For the first time in years, my future felt like something worth anticipating. I spent hours running the numbers, working out the plans I'd need to make that dream come true, and imagining how I'd fill my days once I was finally free of the rat race.

I found peace in establishing new routines that included taking myself on movie date nights every Thursday and long baths with a glass of wine every weekend. For once, life was tranquil, predictable, and safe. I should have known it wouldn't last the moment I met Caleb, my latest trainee, but I had no idea yet that everything was about to change. Again.

Caleb was really something special. At 24, he bore a slight resemblance to Jason Alexander, standing only 5'5" tall, with short, prematurely thinning hair. Privately, I called him Nina, after the woman in *Office Space* who answered the phone with an unbearably cheerful, "Corporate Accounts Payable, Nina speaking. Just a moment." Caleb had the same relentlessly chipper attitude, the kind that bordered on obnoxious.

He had been hired into the same junior role I had started in over a decade before, and it was my job to show him the ropes, walking him through managing the first-tier support tasks. It should've been just another training assignment, another junior technician who would give me a few months or a year's reprieve from that tiresome work before moving on like everyone else had. Everyone except me.

Instead, it was the start of something I *never* saw coming, though in hindsight, I should've seen it from a mile away.

He was so affable that I hated being mad at him. It was tough to hold a grudge against someone who was always happy. He was always quick with a joke or a friendly remark, but he had some infuriating if not confusing quirks that made it almost impossible not to resent it.

Caleb spent much of his time with his feet kicked up on his desk, chatting with a coworker he'd become best buddies with. The impression of his friend's behind is probably still embedded in the cushion of the guest chair in Caleb's old office. From my office directly across the hall, I could overhear just enough of their conversations to catch some dubious tall tales. If he was going to neglect his work in favor of socializing, at least it was entertaining.

The first questionable claim he made was that, before deciding to pursue a career in IT, he had worked as a hairdresser in a salon.

That wouldn't be suspicious in and of itself, except he claimed the name of the salon was "Truvy's," straight out of *Steel Magnolias.*

Another day, after I mentioned having taught some of the chat regulars at The Cabana how to write basic HTML from scratch, he seemed compelled to one-up me. Without explaining what he was supposedly programming, he described a coding mentor who would spend hours at his house coaching him.

"He used to come over and set up his computer right next to mine. We'd spend all night writing code from memory just to see who could fill up the page faster." I still have no idea why he thought that was something programmers would ever do.

The trouble was, Caleb was easily distracted, and the work could be highly detailed and fast-paced. As the queue backed up while he chatted, users who were used to seeing my name in the "assigned to" line of their tickets began calling me to ask about delays or to complain when something wasn't configured correctly.

I didn't want to hound him, especially since I had no authority over him beyond training, but when his fabrications started doubling as excuses for being absent for days at a time, it became a problem.

I'm still bewildered by the biggest whopper Caleb ever told… his excuse for taking two weeks off work. He said his sister's house had been broken into late at night and her infant daughter had been shot in the fray. After the first week, he called in to report that the baby had been in a coma since the incident and the family had decided to pull the plug.

Where he sabotaged himself was in claiming it all happened in a small town about two hours away, as if that explained why he couldn't be at work. He seemed to have forgotten that a tragedy that sensational would have been front-page news in a place that size, making the story easy to verify. There was no mention of it anywhere.

Not wanting to be accused of throwing stones from a glass house especially after my morale hit rock bottom, I refused to call Caleb out for leaving his work undone. It would silently pile up until I'd eventually just give up and do it myself.

To this day, I struggle to reconcile that behavior with my own. When I first stepped into that role, I set extremely high expectations for myself, determined not to let the more senior techs above me feel burdened by the work queues. Few of the people I trained after me seemed to carry that same sense of responsibility, and those who did didn't stay long. It frustrated me that I never felt able to fully let go of that obligation, that I never found a "me" to train whom I could trust to get the job done so I could move on.

More than anything, I felt cheated. I'd paid my dues like those before me. I'd spent years doing the work no one else could tolerate. My diligence had earned them an escape from the work queues, but when it was my turn, the reward was denied.

What made it worse was that the current occupant of Randy's old supervisory position, Pamela, had no intention of correcting Caleb. My elation at finally having another woman on the server team was short-lived as I watched her immediately gravitate toward his infectious personality.

His vivacity won her over until, to her, he could do no wrong. Worse, she started pinning his shortcomings on me. One Saturday I followed a hunch and snuck into the empty office to check my employee file in Pamela's desk. It was thick with notes in her handwriting, faulting me for the ticket backlog, even though keeping the work queue current was Caleb's job. There were no such notes in his file.

If they had their exclusive little club, then the rest of us had ours, grumbling in hushed voices over coffee, trading eye rolls when Pamela camped out in Caleb's office for long stretches. I might've been the only one dealing with the fallout of their friendship directly, but the rest of the team was just as incensed by it. People who normally avoided each other began slipping behind closed doors to commiserate over their common foe.

I had made my own dissatisfaction abundantly clear, spending months openly voicing my discontent and talking very loudly about trying to find another job. Once Pamela lost the need to hide her favoritism, I lost the need to hide my disdain. I started letting it seep into private chat messages to my teammates, knowing full well she'd see it in the logs.

The longer I stayed, the higher the volume of my complaints got, until even the people in the next hallway, who weren't even in our department, started complaining about me. They knew I wasn't happy. Hell, *everyone* knew I wasn't happy. And I knew they weren't happy with me, either.

So it really shouldn't have surprised me when, in January 2020, despite my having over a decade more experience, Caleb was promoted to a lateral position to mine with more pay.

I immediately ramped up my job search, meticulously updating my résumé for each open position I applied for. At first, I kept my search local, hoping to find something nearby so I could stay in my "little cottage" and keep the plans I had made for my future alive. Nothing came up. I expanded the search to Tennessee, thinking maybe it was time to just let it go and go back home.

Still nothing.

As the pressure mounted, I widened my search to include the entire continental United States. Finally, I was offered some interviews.

I interviewed with 10 different teams from every corner of the country, but nothing seemed to fit. Meanwhile, things at work kept deteriorating until I decided I'd rather risk unemployment than stay. I resolved that if I hadn't found something new by the beginning of April, I would give my notice anyway and figure the rest out later. It was a risk I swore I would never take, quitting a job before having another lined up, but I was nearing the end of my rope.

It was almost funny… almost. I had outlasted the worst of the worst, clawing my way through years of being overlooked, underestimated, and shoved aside. And yet, in the end, it wasn't a tyrannical despot who finally broke me. It was an image-obsessed, insecure woman so desperate for a partner-in-crime that she couldn't see past his blatant lies.

Maybe that was the cruelest joke of all. Joke or not, I was done playing… until the COVID pandemic rolled in like a tsunami.

Practically overnight, everything changed. A small group of infrastructure techs were designated as mission-critical staff and kept onsite, while the rest of us were sent to work from home until further notice.

Knowing that, one way or another, I was leaving my job and that it would most likely require a move, I used the unanticipated time at home to start packing and getting the house ready to put on the market. I had no idea where I would end up or how it would affect the long-term plans I had so painstakingly laid out over the last few years. Everything I had envisioned for my future was suddenly in flux.

I had never even worked in another IT shop beyond the one where I had started all those years ago. The idea of stepping into an entirely new environment, with different systems, different expectations, and different people, was both daunting and exhilarating. But one thing was certain: staying wasn't an option.

That decision felt even more justified when we were finally called back to work onsite in June 2020.

Just three days after returning, an email arrived announcing the reconstitution of the Systems Engineering team with new work assignments.

Caleb's promotion hadn't just been a reward for his relentless cheerfulness and ass-kissery skills. It had been a setup, a strategically laid path leading straight to the Systems Engineering team into the exact spot I had been working toward for more than a decade.

To make matters worse, they eliminated his first-tier position, and permanently reassigned me back to the first-tier support queue. It was a quiet demotion, but everyone could see what they had done. It wasn't just humiliating, it reversed my career, freezing me in place back where I started. I'd landed on Park Place and ended up in jail anyway. I didn't even get to collect my $200.

Then, just two hours after the announcement landed, like divine intervention breaking through the clouds, an email arrived in my personal inbox during lunch.

A job offer. Not just any offer, a bona fide senior systems administrator position with a 30% raise that would finally propel me past every coworker who'd spent years leapfrogging over me, catching me up to where I should've been all along in one fell swoop.

All I had to do was move to Arizona.

Done.

I submitted my notice before the end of the day.

Chapter 22: Reduction Enforced

I've never been a particularly well-traveled person. School trips and family vacations carried me up and down the eastern side of the continent, from the bustling streets of Toronto to the sunbaked sprawl of Florida's beaches, but I hadn't ventured farther west than New Orleans until I moved to Arizona.

I'd had it drilled into me by the heavy-handed managers at my early, pre-career jobs that taking time off was a selfish act, an unnecessary burden placed on my coworkers even if I had earned the time off. So, I just never did it. Working for the consulting firm in South Carolina only reinforced that mindset. I was on-call 24/7 for most of those years, tethered to my phone like a '90s TV doctor with a pager. If George Clooney had been on our team, it would've at least been tolerable.

I was supposed to stay within a two-hour driving distance of the office in case of an emergency. I shouldn't have even risked the Saturday day trips to the coast for an occasional beach day, but I loved having my perspective adjusted by the vastness of the open sea. If I ever felt overwhelmed, I could make my troubles feel insignificant simply by gazing out over the edge of the world.

By the time I finally accepted the position in Arizona, I had racked up over a year's worth of unused leave. That reserve became my ticket out. I took a full month off before closing out my tenure, and the payout from the remainder of my leave was enough to fund my entire move.

Now, I was perched in the cab of a 26-foot moving truck, headed west past the Mighty Mississip' for the first time at the age of 45, with everything I owned packed into the cargo box behind me.

I didn't know what to expect. I knew it would be different, but I could do different. Moving from Knoxville to Columbia had been a shock to the system, and I'd survived that just fine. But nothing could have prepared me for the seismic shift of moving to Arizona. Something about it knocked the breath out of me. I thought of all the vain effort I'd poured into trying to find work near home in East Tennessee, where at least I understood the curves in the road and the cadence of the people.

"I'm going to hate it here," I whimpered out loud to an empty truck cab. Somehow, in all the rush to move, I had forgotten to research my new home beyond what little I knew from job listings. I didn't realize how expansive it was. I had never lived in a city with a population over 200,000 before, and now I was barreling toward a sprawling metropolis with millions of people and traffic patterns that could frighten the warts off a frog.

As it turns out, the old adage is right. You can take the girl out of the country, but you can't take the country out of the girl. And the Appalachian part? That's even more stubborn.

My new job wasn't anything I hadn't seen before, and I genuinely appreciated the freedom that the COVID-era telework policies provided during that first year. I used the time to keep an eye on the real estate listings from my personal computer during lunch breaks, comparing each new property to a long wish list of features and researching neighborhoods. Despite the havoc of the pandemic housing market, I somehow managed to buy a new home within nine months of arriving in town.

The equity I'd cashed out of the South Carolina house gave me the ability to shop for homes far beyond anything I'd ever dreamed of. I made an offer on a house in a neighborhood with a familiar vibe, like the one I used to dream about living in as a kid. It had been where my parents took us on Halloween to trick-or-treat when we were growing up in the country, and this neighborhood had the same soul. It was built in the '70s around a country club, the kind of place that reminded me of where Ally's family lived in *The Karate Kid*.

It was the first property I had ever purchased entirely on my own, which only made the moment more surreal. All I could think was, *so they're just going to hand me the keys and let me have it now?!*

I finally understood why people say that same thing about bringing newborns home from the hospital. Now, at over 50, I still don't feel like a grownup, certainly not someone who just goes out and purchases whole houses, and definitely not ones with in-ground pools.

I'd only been in the new house a month when the company decided COVID telework was over. I knew I'd been forced to move to the city where the headquarters were for a reason, but the server team manager had been certain he could get permanent telework approved before we were recalled. Most of the company's departments had underperformed during the pandemic, but ours had excelled. Nevertheless, just as I was getting used to spending an hour after work in the pool before dinner, I suddenly found myself spending it in a hot car instead.

The transition was brutal.

I was back in a cube farm for the first time after having enjoyed the comfort of a private office for most of my 18 years with the consulting firm, and then working from home for over a year. I hadn't realized how much I'd outgrown the lack of privacy in shared spaces until I found myself shoved right back into one.

I could no longer tolerate people walking up behind me out of nowhere or the team congregating in the cubes nearby to have boisterous conversations about weekend activities. The constant movement and overlapping voices triggered full-blown panic attacks, the kind that sent me bolting into the hallway where I'd stand listening to my pounding heart while I waited for the gathering to disperse.

Noise-canceling headphones didn't cover it well enough. Worse, using them too much was starting to piss off management. I had flashbacks to my old cube at the media company and pondered how I'd managed back then, situated next to the conference room door with my back to a high-traffic area.

The 30-minute lunch break wasn't long enough to run out for food, so I'd sit in my car and try to steal a quick nap to avoid the break room social trap. It was just as well. I needed it to stop my eyes from burning. No matter what tricks I tried, I just could *not* fall asleep before 1 a.m., still every bit as much of a night owl as I was back in the chat room days. It left me with four hours of sleep at best, once I factored in the time it took to get ready and commute across the city for a surprisingly early start time that turned out to be militantly inflexible.

To make matters worse, the building had no Wi-Fi and no cell service. The bathrooms stunk. The long, hot walk in from the parking lot two blocks away stunk even more. And then there was the man who defied established office etiquette by microwaving fish on a weekly basis. To be fair, he did ask if it was bothersome, but everyone was too polite to admit it was. Regardless of what anyone tells you, the answer to that question is *always* "yes."

What made it all worse was knowing none of it was necessary. I hadn't lost the comfort of my home office because the job demanded it, I'd lost it because people resented that others got to stay home when they couldn't. It turned out that our supervisor's boss had been given the discretion to let us continue teleworking while others were ordered back, but he refused.

"I'm lonely when everyone's working from home," he would say, or "must be nice to be off all the time," thoughtlessly dismissing all of the output that had been produced from our homes as if none of it had mattered. In truth, he wanted to be able to watch us come and go from his corner office windows, complaining to our supervisors if anyone arrived late or left early by even five minutes.

I longed for the days when I joked about not knowing how my coworkers kept their jobs, constantly producing HR violations. "They keep jumping up on my desk naked to wave their bare backsides in my face," I reported to the team's group chat. Add missing my pets to the daily drudgery of onsite work, I guess.

Miserable and increasingly on edge, I started applying to every remote position I could find, desperately hoping *something* would break through before I completely lost my ever-loving mind.

I began to fantasize about moving to a small town back east, somewhere closer to home and far away from the constant buzz of city life. And I already knew just the place. Nestled among the red clay earth and kudzu just south of Atlanta is the little town of Senoia, Georgia, where *The Walking Dead* had been filmed.

I first visited in 2015, treating myself to a solo driving tour of the show's filming locations as a distraction after the breakup. It was something I had been wanting to do since the show began in 2010, but I had been watching my marriage slowly die instead. The moment I drove onto Main Street, I accidentally fell head over heels in love with the place.

After that first visit, I made a point to take a mini-vacation there every year until I left for Arizona. I'd stay at the big bed-and-breakfast in town and spend a few peaceful days wandering the charming downtown area on foot, trading rush hour congestion for peaceful strolls past the quaint storefronts of antique shops and locally owned eateries.

I daydreamed about owning a little local artists' boutique on the same block as the coffee and ice cream shops, chatting with familiar faces every morning and having lunch at Matt's Smalltown Pizza once a week as if I were an area native.

I had seen the filming locations, eaten at the same restaurants the show's cast visited, and watched production assistants shuttle costumed extras to set, but that wasn't why I kept coming back. In fact, the production had become more of a nuisance than an attraction. Whenever production vans were parked outside the "Gin Property," a neighborhood that made up the Alexandria set across the train track from Main Street, the little town filled up with gawkers until there was no parking to be had anywhere nearby.

The town had all the best hallmarks of home: a similar climate, familiar culture, and the same flora and fauna I'd grown up with. I craved it constantly when I was back in my real life. It was like someone had taken the feeling of decompression and created a place with it. It was *better* than going home.

I'd started imagining Senoia as my permanent home back when I was plotting out my retirement before leaving South Carolina. I pictured buying a small house on one of those tranquil streets, a modest "forever home" from which I'd never have to move again. A fully remote job could make that dream a reality years earlier than I'd ever imagined. So when I interviewed for a virtualization tech position, I made sure to ask if I'd be permitted to move after accepting the job.

"Oh, it shouldn't be a problem," they assured me, "The role is fully remote. Our team doesn't even have an office at headquarters."

If I landed that job, yet *another* pop culture moment would steer my life in a surprising new direction.

I wasn't going to be sad to leave Arizona after only three years. I wasn't cut out for desert life, and it hadn't been the dream job I'd hoped for. I had effectively turned into an overqualified secretary for the team, managing spreadsheets instead of servers unless there was something unpleasant no one else wanted to deal with.

I had asked during the interview if there would be after-hours work, hoping to ensure my weekends would be safe for the first time in 13 years. They laughed and assured me they weren't approved for it, which left me giddy at the thought of leaving it behind. I had already relocated for the job when I realized they thought I had been asking about overtime pay to earn extra money. Once I got there, I discovered that not only was there after-hours work, but I was required to forfeit one Saturday a month to it.

After weeks of savoring the idea of my first strictly Monday-through-Friday, eight-to-five job in over a decade, I was furious. On the Saturdays I had to log in by 7 a.m., I spent the entire day seething with anger, livid that I'd fallen for yet another bait-and-switch. My relationship with my new neighbors never recovered once they overheard my early-morning ranting about it through my home office window. The wife uncomfortably avoided eye contact and scuttled away every time we accidentally walked out to the curb at the same time on trash day.

The Return to Office mandate was just the last straw. When the offer for the new remote position arrived, there was no question I'd accept, even though it didn't come with a raise. In fact, I'd lose all of my accrued leave, have to change healthcare providers, and have to start all over with nothing, yet again.

I submitted my request to move to Senoia within a month of starting my new job, but my excitement faded as I watched it stir up a familiar old song and dance. Just like in South Carolina when I was trying to land my first IT job, HR kept kicking it back, asking for more justification and more documentation.

As an employee hired under a remote-work agreement, my location wouldn't have mattered except it was right in the middle of what felt like a national push to get the entire country back onsite after everyone had collectively decided the pandemic was over. Private sector CEOs became just as infatuated with dragging everyone back to the office as their public sector counterparts. I could keep my remote-work agreement if I stayed, but if I wanted to move, it would have to be to a city where the company had a field office I could work in. Eventually, I had to admit what was becoming obvious. I was stuck in Arizona.

At least I was still working from home, even if I wasn't where I wanted to be. If I had to, I could stick it out until retirement and make my way back east then. I had just enough time left to make the financials work, so long as I stuck it out and stopped job-hopping long enough to become fully vested in my new retirement account.

By autumn of 2024, more than a year had passed since I started the new job, almost without me realizing it. I'd just been trudging along, learning new skills at work and going through my usual seasonal rituals at home. Before I knew it, pumpkin spice lattes and jack-o-lanterns were back, and I was already planning how I was going to decorate for Christmas.

I should've known better by now: peace never lasts long in my life. For someone who would sooner eat a flaming dog turd than intentionally stir up drama, it's always been a sore spot. Every time I think the turmoil is gone, it comes roaring back with a vengeance. And this time, it wasn't just about me.

The prior summer had been refreshingly uplifting. I'd never considered myself a Taylor Swift fan, but lounging by the pool watching clips of her record-smashing Eras Tour on my phone all season put me in full-on girl-power mode. Not only had Taylor taken over social media, but Chappell Roan's songs "Pink Pony Club" and "Femininomenon" were everywhere. At work, I had also somehow found myself on a systems administration team with five other women, so my whole world seemed poised to shift toward embracing the feminine. I felt uplifted and hopeful for the first time in a long time.

But as summer came to an end, that brightness slipped away. The tour came to a close after nearly two years of shows, and the harshness of winter settled in, replacing the summer's optimism with a renewed sense of upheaval. I just didn't expect how quickly the tone changed.

I'm not sure *what* I expected, but it wasn't this.

Stories of companies cutting Christmas bonuses at the last minute and freezing supply orders hit the newswires like an avalanche. Businesses that had only caught a faint whiff of sulfur in the air were suddenly dragging out fire trucks, desperate to douse anything that might spark a blaze in their bottom lines. Everyone was talking about layoffs… mass layoffs across every sector.

My teammates and I were told to expect a reduction in force. Supervisors whispered to those on the cusp of retirement that they might want to consider throwing themselves on the grenade, to retire early and save one of us from the axe. And, as if the anti-telework sentiment had become as infectious as COVID, our remote-work agreements were revoked without warning.

I was forced to report to work in a small regional field office that had nothing to do with my job, sharing a small room with a man who worked in an entirely different department. Still, as angry as I was for being forced back into an office when I had planned never to work in one again, I counted my blessings. It wasn't nearly as uncomfortable as the last office had been. My roommate spent a fair amount of time out in the field, so I had part-time privacy and cell reception, at least.

I looked around and couldn't believe how I got here, how all my plans had suddenly gone awry. A layoff was almost a certainty now. If it happened, I didn't have the time left to financially recover and retire on time… and even worse… I could bury any hope I had left of living in Senoia at all. But that was the least of my worries.

For months we watched as people reported having applied for dozens or even hundreds of jobs without finding work. Thousands of federal employees had flooded the job market, and thousands more private sector employees were right on their heels. Everyone knew that anyone who lost their job now wouldn't find another one for a very long time. Even more damning, losing an IT job and having a long break in employment right in the middle of an AI boom would leave me behind technologically. Would my skills even be marketable after a year of unemployment in this fast evolving field?

This wasn't just about losing my retirement anymore, this was about losing the career I had fought for, the one I battled through raging anxiety, and stood against misogynists and screaming department heads for. I didn't have a support system to lean on anymore, either. I didn't know what would happen to me if I lost my ability to pay my bills. I would have nowhere to go. I couldn't imagine the choices I might have to make. If my ship was going down, would I get to the lifeboats in time, or would I still be clinging to the stern's railing as it plunged into the darkness?

Worst of all, I couldn't see my future anymore.

Within the space of just a few months, I had gone from blissfully believing that I was within arm's reach of a dream retirement, to contemplating the unthinkable.

Walking into work every day felt like stepping into the final dinner scene in *Don't Look Up*. Each of us clung to the last vestiges of routine while pretending everything was fine, nervously searching each other's demeanor for an unspoken reassurance that no one had to give.

No one knew what was coming, but the one thing we all could agree upon was that whatever it was, it wasn't going to be good.

I must've wondered more times than I could ever count what my father would say if he suddenly appeared in front of me. I never doubted he'd be proud, I only wondered if I could make it show on his face. Could I coax that impish grin back out by telling him how a celebrity crush set me on a lifelong path in technology? Or how I'd stood my ground when everything seemed stacked against me? Would he flip a table and shout, "After everything she's done to earn this, *this* is how it ends?!"

And with that image in my mind, I eased my laptop shut with a soft click. Sliding my reading glasses up to my forehead, I pinched the bridge of my nose as my eyes blurred with tears.

"Yeah. This is how it ends."

Postscript

I began writing this book in February 2025 as a way to cope with the mayhem exploding around me. Faced with the possibility of losing my career, I found myself reflecting on how I got here in the first place.

For years, I avoided telling my Blungo story. Even after all this time, it felt like a violation of trust, maybe even exploitation. And I won't lie, part of me worried it just sounded goofy. Especially after I mentioned it once on social media and someone commented, "I don't know if this is cringe or hilarious."

But the truth is, it happened. And it happened to me, a nobody from Tennessee who found herself in the middle of Leomania with a story nobody else had. In the moment, it was thrilling. It was delightfully twisted. And it mattered, even if only to me.

On its own, maybe it wasn't enough to fill a memoir. But when I stepped back and looked at how my career unfolded, I realized I'd been wrong about that. The story of Blungo, *Titanic*, and the story of how I built my life, they aren't separate. They're inextricably linked.

Once I started writing, once I began weaving my story through pop culture and technology, with Leo and Blungo not just fitting into it but acting as a catalyst for everything that followed, I knew I'd finally found the right way to tell it. If I were ever going to do this, it had to be *now*. And it had to be *this* way.

I've always dreamed of writing a book, but every other attempt had ended in spectacular disappointment. I'm definitely not a fiction writer, that much is certain. It took years for it to click that I had a story of my own worth telling. After all, I'm just one insignificant voice rising, briefly, from the burbling cacophony of the masses. But maybe that's the point. We all have stories to tell, and we all have more in common than we like to admit. This one just happens to be mine, and maybe it's not unique. Maybe that's what makes it worth sharing.

If you've made it this far, if you're still here, reading, then I've triumphed, at long last. It means I've successfully brought you along for the entire journey, not just Blungo's leg of the trip but my whole odyssey. Almost.

I had one final phone call with Kim after Gary died, when she happened upon his obituary and called me at work.

When I explained what happened, she apologized for setting us up over a decade earlier. She hadn't realized how easily his character would crumble and felt responsible. I reassured her that he'd duped us all because, of course, there was much more to that story that I haven't shared here and will never share publicly.

It was during that call that she dropped one last plot twist.

She claimed to have evidence, though in classic Kim fashion, she wouldn't say what it was, that Matthew and Tiffany had never been real. According to her, they were a figment of Gwen's imagination.

I remembered seeing the photographs "they" had sent Kim, pinned to the wall above her computer when I visited her. Even then, something about them had struck me as off. Kim raved about how beautiful Tiffany was, with her soft natural blonde curls. To me, they looked *too* perfect, like models in the placeholder photos that come in a Dollar General frame.

As it turns out, they probably were. I kicked myself for never realizing how unlikely it would have been in 1999, before widespread use of Wi-Fi or cable internet, that both of them would be on separate computers in the same house, both connected to the internet and both chatting at the same time. It was far more likely in those days to have been one person with multiple browser windows open, logged into the chat room under different names.

Even now, I struggle to understand what the motivation could have been. Maybe it was a former Paradise Island regular trying to ease their guilt by making sure my new chat room looked like a success. Or maybe they were simply Gwen's extroverted alter egos.

To be honest, I'd rather she hadn't told me. That shadow of doubt over something I once held as real cast an unwelcome pall over my memories of those days. But in the grand scheme of things, what difference does it make now?

I do, however, find it amusing that there seems to be more solid evidence Matthew and Tiffany were catfish than there ever was that Blungo was.

I've never liked talking about how going to see *Titanic* that day changed everything. It always sounded like the kind of thing a star-struck fan might say to their favorite actor, something that would make them uncomfortable, unsure how to respond. But here I am. I've done it. I've not just said it, but written an entire book about it. And, at least for me, it's not mere flattery.

I think it would have taken me much longer to leave my first marriage if Rose and Jack hadn't inspired me to go sooner. I wouldn't have started building Leo fan sites. I never would have met Kim on one, and without her I wouldn't have met or married Husband v2.0, discovered the "joys" of a career in Information Technology, or found my way west in pursuit of it.

I have no assumptions about whether Leo will ever read this book, beyond assuming he won't, but I'll admit that I hope, one day, he will. If he is reading this now, with no expectations or supposition, I just want to say:

Thank you.

The characters you brought to life, both in Jack Dawson and in your public persona, inspired a domino effect that steered my life and career almost as much as it did yours, just in a much quieter way. It may have been a shit-fight every step of the way after that, but it's been my life, every last bitter second of it.

If "Blungo" *wasn't* you, he was an impressive fake, convincing enough to fool even a cautious old skeptic like me. Unfortunately, he was also more than likely a friend of yours, someone I'd be tempted to write a book just to get your attention to warn you about, had it not all happened so long ago. Thankfully, that wasn't necessary.

If he *was* you and anything I described from those days embarrassed you, just remember—we were all young and a little bit stupid, and at least *you've* still got plausible deniability. I'd be genuinely surprised if you remember anything beyond vague recollections of being in someone's chat room, but I hope I've lived up to the trust you placed in me all those years ago either way.

And congratulations on finally getting that goddamn Oscar.

I'm proud of you.

"After everything, I still believe in paradise. Not as a place, but as the rare moment when you know, without question, you belong. Once you've experienced it, the memory of it never fades with the years; it echoes within you for the rest of your days."

—S. Ashbaine
inspired by
Richard's final speech in
The Beach (2000 film)

One More Thing:

The Tale of the Vanishing Cheez Balls

A Short Story

While I was living in the little apartment where I ran The Cabana chat room and participated in the O Chats before Blungo disappeared into the ether, something happened that had absolutely nothing to do with any of that. It didn't fit anywhere in my memoir, but I still think about it often, first with amusement… and then in utter horror.

While all of this was going on, I had embarked on a yearlong weight-loss journey. Every day after work, I'd come home, lace up my sneakers, and run to the end of my road and back. I had lost a significant amount of weight and was feeling pretty proud of myself, but the cravings for the very foods that caused the issue were still as strong as ever.

One of my favorite guilty pleasures had always been Planters Cheez Balls, the kind in the blue cardboard canister. My penchant for rewarding myself for dieting success by sabotaging that success never ceases to amaze me, but I brought home a brand-new can as a special treat one afternoon.

Sitting at my desk in the back spare room chatting away, I opened the foil seal and took a single handful of the unnaturally orange snack, snapped the yellow plastic lid back on, and gently placed the can next to my monitor. I can still see it sitting there in my mind's eye, even today. I promised myself not to touch them again until the next day. The kind of restraint I had back then completely eludes me now.

I sat at my desk in the media office all day the next day, my mouth watering at the thought of another handful of the treats. That night, I donned my shoes as usual and, upon my return from my jog, settled at my desk ready to pop open the canister as the modem dialed out with that familiar screech. But as I reached for the can, I realized it was gone.

Gone? I blinked, then looked again. *Gone!*

"But I'm the only one who lives here!"

I had moved in unexpectedly, the same day the landlord had agreed to give me the apartment without a deposit or upfront rent. When I had arrived, neither my apartment nor the one next door had a lock. I ran to the hardware store to buy one as my friends and family moved my things, and had given Brenda the only other key.

Not even the landlord had one.

"Were you in my apartment today?" I grilled her. She emphatically denied the allegation, insisting she had no reason to enter my private lair. I tore that apartment apart, looking behind every piece of furniture, under the bed, and even under the heap of clothes and accessories at the bottom of my closet.

Nothing.

In a last-ditch attempt to preserve my sanity, I even walked down to the dumpster at the far side of the parking lot, almost hoping I would find it there in a freshly tossed garbage bag. Sleep-eating, then walking the evidence down the stairs, across the parking lot, and back, only to return to bed without any memory of it, somehow seemed more plausible than *"I guess they just disappeared."*

Even as I packed up to move out of state two years later, I kept an eye out for a moldy, repulsive can of Planters Cheez Balls, but they never materialized.

Decades passed, and the mystery of the Cheez Balls lingered. I laughed it off, claiming it must have been my father who had a known *hankering for a hunk o' cheese* at all times. Still, had his ghost taken the whole canister as a joke? I could certainly fathom him eating the delectable puffs themselves, but taking the can, too? That was one bridge too far.

A few years ago, as I mulled over "The Cheez Balls Incident" yet again, I remembered something that sent a shockwave through me.

One day, as I went to get my shoes from the bedroom closet for my daily jog, I noticed a bit of pink insulation on the carpet in front of the closet doorway. *Strange, the new landlord must've been in the attic doing repairs and opened the attic access door above the closet for some reason,* I thought, naively.

The apartment next door was still vacant.
It still did not have a lock on the door.
And it, too, had an attic access panel in the bedroom closet.

My chin practically melted to the floor as I realized in abject terror, decades after the fact, that someone had broken into my apartment through the attic while I was at work. They could have been covertly living in the apartment next door without my knowledge for weeks, watching me, waiting for me to leave, entering my apartment whenever they were reasonably sure I would be at work all day.

They must have been homeless, hungry. Had they asked, I would have given them the can. But considering I left the closet door open all the time, they could have silently lifted the access panel and watched me in my bedroom and I would have never known. That is the stuff nightmares are made of, and I only noticed 20-some-odd years later because I've never forgotten that damn can of Planters Cheez Balls.

Sleep well, friends.

Thank you for reading my memoir.

I would love to hear what you thought of it. Please consider leaving a short review at your favorite book retailer, or send me a private note at Susan@SusanAshbaine.com. What do *you* think? Was it him, or wasn't it?

For updates & bonus content, visit the
author's website: www.SusanAshbaine.com

Appendix: Extra Bits & Bytes

This memoir was written as a personal story, not a documentary record. To keep the narrative moving, I sometimes simplified timelines, compressed events, or left out technical details that would have slowed the pacing. The notes that follow offer additional context for readers who are curious about what happened behind the scenes. They clarify where the story diverges from day-to-day reality and provide a few factual details that didn't fit naturally into the flow of the chapters. None of these notes change the heart of the story; they're here as background for those who want to peek "behind the screens" or for those who were there and might be wondering why it seems different than you recall.

On the Cabana and Thai Kids

About halfway through the "Blungo" experience, Richard replaced the InsideTheWeb message boards on the Thai Kid's site with a proper forum system that had a built-in chat room. At that point, the Cabana closed and our regulars transitioned to the chat room on the Thai Kid's site, where the last half of the Blungo story actually occurred. For the sake of simplicity, I left the story in The Cabana for the duration.

On Paradise Isle

When the original Paradise Isle was unveiled, it was an almost one-to-one duplicate of my Paradise Island site. At some point afterward, the webmasters replaced it with a vastly different design which is likely what most longer-term regulars there will remember. It is not my intent to claim they used my design permanently.

On Composite Characters

This book contains several composite characters, each drawn from the traits and actions of two or three real people. Most of what is described of them did occur, but often years earlier or involving different people than the characters represent. I needed to tell a story that included complex or sensitive situations while still respecting privacy and the careers of those still active in the workforce. To do so, I simply drew inspiration from past experiences to stand in for those later scenarios.

On the Accuracy of the Chat Detail

A few of the chat conversations surrounding Blungo's visits in The Cabana (and later Richard's chat room) were lightly constructed to provide context for individual one-line quotes I remember vividly. The quotes themselves, however, are as accurate as memory allows. All of the dialogue attributed to Blungo, including "The T-Shirt Question" chat, is a direct point-for-point recollection, though it may not be verbatim.

On Blungo's Real Identity

I have never definitively claimed that Leonardo DiCaprio was "Blungo," and I have never attempted to contact him or his team (as of this writing) to seek verification. I remain hopeful that he may one day reach out and settle the question, but if he does, whether that information becomes public will be entirely his decision. "Blungo," of course, was not the actual handle my anonymous friend used, so even if it was him, Leo would not acknowledge use of that pseudonym.

www.ingramcontent.com/pod-product-compliance
Lightning Source LLC
LaVergne TN
LVHW090106250926
848814LV00049B/54/J
* 9 7 9 8 3 3 0 4 4 8 3 8 8 *